Who picks you up when you're down and need someone?

Whom do you trust the most with a burning secret you need to share? Who would never tell another soul?

Who gives you advice if you're having problems with a colleague at work?

Who is the first person you call when you want to go out, relax, and have a good time?

Who will sit down and truly listen to every word you say when you want to share a story?

Who knows how to push you to do more — to achieve more?

Who always seems to anticipate what you're going to say next — before the words even leave your mouth?

Who would stick up for you at work if your job were on the line?

Who runs around telling others how great you are?

*Who are your **Vital Friends**?*

VITAL
FRIENDS

THE PEOPLE
YOU CAN'T AFFORD TO
LIVE WITHOUT

VITAL
FRIENDS

TOM RATH

GALLUP PRESS
New York

GALLUP PRESS
1251 Avenue of the Americas
23rd Floor
New York, NY 10020

Library of Congress Control Number: 2006923393
ISBN-10: 1-59562-007-9
ISBN-13: 978-1-59562-007-1

First Printing: 2006
10 9 8 7 6 5 4 3 2 1

— to Ashley, my Energizer for eternity

CONTENTS

SOMETHING'S MISSING

The energy *between* two people is what creates great marriages, families, teams, and organizations.

Yet when we think consciously about improving our lives, we put almost all of our effort into *self*-development.

As I look back on my formal education, it was based almost entirely on mastery of a topic or building *my* knowledge base. In grade school, I learned how to read, multiply, and write, and I struggled to grasp a foreign language. During college and graduate school, I had the opportunity to focus on even more specific topics that piqued *my* interest. Throughout my professional life, I have attended countless development programs that aimed to make *me* more productive.

Even when I have dedicated time to developing others, my attention has focused on each person's *self*-development.

I had it all wrong. The potential was hiding *within* each relationship in my life.

— *Tom Rath*

PART ONE:
FRIENDS IN LIFE

CHAPTER 1:
WHO EXPECTS YOU TO BE SOMEBODY?

"How did you end up on the streets?"

Roger, a big burly man, sat in silence and stared at me, a nervous, skinny interviewer with wire-rimmed glasses. He thought about the question for a few minutes, the words echoing through his head as he searched for a response. Seated in a chair three feet in front of him, I eagerly awaited his reply.

Roger scratched his head and caught me glancing at his hand. His rough, leathery skin had clearly endured the elements during the two decades he had been on the streets. His nails were caked with dirt, and his hollow eyes revealed an emptiness that I could see even before I asked the first question. Roger described to me the great life he once had. He had grown up in a wonderful home, was married right after graduating from college, found a job with a respectable mechanical engineering firm, bought a house and two cars, and had three children by the age of 30. To my surprise, Roger had lived a very "normal" life.

Then, Roger explained to me what had happened so many years ago to change all that. He described how his frustration at work was increasing each day. His only real friend at work, Jimmy, had been fired. Aside from his wife, Jimmy was Roger's best friend in the world. They joined a bowling league together, went on hunting trips every November, and their families were close. Roger and Jimmy had offices right next to each other, and they talked every day — not just about work, but about personal matters as well. Their friendship kept both men engaged in a job that would have otherwise been dreary. Since Jimmy's termination, Roger could hardly muster the motivation to go to work.

For eight years, Roger and Jimmy were forced to tolerate the same boss, Mike, a hostile man who took every opportunity to remind his employees how much seniority he had with the company. Mike would belittle Roger, Jimmy, and other employees at every turn. As Roger described Mike, you could tell that he was one of those managers whose abrasive demeanor inflicted damage far beyond the nine-to-five workday. When Roger recounted stories about Mike, his jaw tightened, and he raised his lower lip into a scowl. He seemed to be seething with hatred.

Roger's peers at work didn't make the situation any better — they all suffered through Mike's abuse in stoic silence. After Jimmy was fired, Roger was left with his boss and a few other engineers who didn't say much. They rarely socialized on the job. Everyone was simply punching a clock at work, eager to get out of there at the end of the day.

By the time Roger finished work each evening, he needed an escape. So he began drinking. At first, Roger stopped by the neighborhood bar one or two nights a week. Soon, that became five or six nights of heavy drinking. Even though his family tried hard to reverse his downward spiral, he began to self-destruct.

As Roger described his wife's efforts to help, the pain in his voice spoke volumes. He could not bring himself to call her by name during our interview, nor did he ever mention his children's names. At the age of 32, Roger had lost his job, his wife, and his children. He had moved into a small apartment. For six months, his mother paid his rent and tried desperately to help him. Roger continued to push her away. Like the others, she eventually gave up on him out of frustration.

Left with no means of support, Roger was forced to live in his car. One day, he returned from his daily journey scrounging for food and found that even his meager home was gone. The police had impounded his car because of back taxes and unpaid parking tickets. Roger was officially homeless for the first time in his life.

Roger recounted this last part of the story in a dry, matter-of-fact tone. I could tell that the real turning points — the moments that had scarred his memory for 20 years — were Roger's final conversations with friends and loved ones. Once the relationships were broken, little else mattered.

As Roger finished his lengthy reply to my question, he could sense that the interview was drawing to a close. But I had one last question:

"Who expects you to be somebody?"

Roger paused for a moment, took a deep breath, and said, "I don't think anyone does anymore."

PROJECT RECOVERY

In 1991, I was invited to work on a special research study on homelessness. The project's aim was to help shelters and city missions develop better programs for people in need. My assignment, in partnership with several other researchers, was to conduct a series of interviews. Armed with our questions and tape recorders, we visited homeless shelters, city missions, and gathering places for the needy. Over the span of four months, we interviewed hundreds of men and women around the country. Our goal was to answer one main question:

Why do some people emerge from homelessness and recover, while others do not?

To answer this question, we started by interviewing people who were homeless and not headed toward recovery (according to experts in each community). My initial suspicion, likely rooted in age-old stereotypes, was that most homeless men and women were in their situation as a result of extreme alcohol or drug abuse. So we asked several questions designed to uncover such dependencies. Sure enough, many of the people I spoke with had severe addictions, and some suffered from serious mental illnesses.

But as I listened closely, it was clear that alcoholism or a dependency on methamphetamines was more of a symptom than a root cause. In most cases, the relationship with a bottle or needle was precipitated by the collapse of a close relationship with a friend or loved one. The men and women who remained homeless for decades had something in common: a lack of healthy friendships. They were more "friendshipless" than anything else — being without a home was just the most obvious and visible part of their plight. By no means was this the only reason people ended up on the streets, but it was one common theme I heard throughout these interviews.

After studying why people wind up homeless, we turned our attention to those who had emerged from homelessness and had recovered. We wanted to figure out what enables people to conquer homelessness. To do so, we contacted directors of city missions and shelters, asking if they knew of people who had been homeless at one point, but were now employed, living on their own, and generally doing well.

Tracking down people in this group posed a real challenge. They were hard to find, and some had extremely busy schedules. One by one, we arranged for telephone interviews. Then we asked a series of questions to identify men and women who had truly recovered. A woman I will call "Maggie" was among the people I spoke with in this recovery group.

Maggie never had much of a chance growing up. She didn't know her biological father, and she was not even sure her mother knew who he was. When Maggie was young, her mother bounced from one abusive relationship to the next. Each man who entered her home seemed to make things worse. And her mother, whom Maggie regarded as a terribly needy woman, spent her life doing anything she could to please her men, even if it meant ignoring the damage they inflicted on Maggie.

Most of the men were just rude to Maggie or ignored her. At least two of them hit her. And then, when Maggie was 16, "Stepdad #4" crossed the line. One day, he cornered Maggie, wrapped his "flabby, tattooed arms" around her small frame, and tried to kiss her. She managed to get away and went directly to her mother and told her what happened, still shaken from the incident. As Maggie might have expected, her mother refused to believe her. She stood behind her man, not her daughter. That was the last time Maggie spoke to her mother.

For the next six years, Maggie was on her own. At first, she stayed with a classmate, then at a local center for runaway teens. Eventually, she spent her nights on the street. In her mind, life on the street was better than living with her "shell of a mother" and the abuse at home.

During this time, Maggie frequented DayHouse, a shelter for homeless people. DayHouse always had a few volunteers on hand — usually young people determined to change the world — who ended up serving mashed potatoes to those who would rather not talk. One of the volunteers, Jessica, took a particular interest in Maggie.

Every Friday, when Jessica volunteered at DayHouse, she tried to initiate a conversation with Maggie. At first, Maggie was skeptical and didn't say much. She figured this short, stocky, warm-faced college girl was like the others. Maggie could tell that some of the students at DayHouse were volunteering to pad their résumés, to please their parents, or to meet a school requirement. But Jessica continued to try, and Maggie started to sense her genuine warmth — something the kids who were in it for themselves lacked.

Over the next 18 months, even though her formal volunteer time had ended, Jessica continued to visit Maggie. Some days, they would just spend time together and talk. Other times, Jessica would come in filled with ideas about how she could help Maggie get a job and help her with mock job interviews. When Maggie secured a real interview, Jessica insisted on taking her shopping so she would have something decent to wear.

Recounting their first outing together, Maggie became emotional as she described what happened when they bumped into one of Jessica's classmates at a department store. After exchanging the usual pleasantries, Jessica said, "This is my friend Maggie." Not only had these words been seared into Maggie's memory for good, but I could tell they had given her even more motivation.

It ended up taking almost two years, but with Jessica's help, Maggie found a job. She started out as a receptionist at an accounting firm, quickly learned the business, and soon thereafter had enough money to rent an apartment. A few years later, Maggie earned a degree and became an auditor. By her own admission, Maggie might not have been the most outgoing "people person" like Jessica, but she had a way with numbers and enjoyed her job. She loved the analytical work, and she was on the way to being remarkably successful.

When I called to conduct my telephone interview with Maggie, it was 10 years after she landed her first job at that accounting firm. She described how she had found a profession she loved — and worked very hard to prove herself. Maggie knew that people were watching her closely, given her exceptional turnaround story, and they had high expectations. This fueled her drive to accomplish even more. At the time of our interview, Maggie was an executive at a major financial services company and earning a sizeable income.

Most importantly, Maggie was very happy with her life and had started a family of her own. She had a loving husband, a two-year-old daughter, and a newborn son. And Maggie's network of friendships was thriving.

When I asked Maggie, *"Who expects you to be somebody?"* her response, like Roger's, was clear and to the point.

"Jessica."

CHAPTER 2:
THE ENERGY *BETWEEN*

As the divergent stories of Roger and Maggie illustrate, friendships are among *the* most fundamental of human needs. The fact is, we are biologically predisposed to this need for relationships, and our environment accentuates this every day. Without friends, it is very difficult for us to get by, let alone thrive.

That's why it's troubling to see that the vast majority of human study has focused on either individuals or groups, not on one-on-one relationships:

- Most psychologists focus on individuals.

- Sociologists tend to study groups.

- Anthropologists primarily explore our roots.

Newer, more application-oriented fields like organizational development look at individuals, work teams, and companies as basic units of study. The study of social networks focuses on all of the interconnections within a group, but it does not dedicate as much time to the intricacies of a single relationship between two people.

Thousands of books and professional development programs explore leadership, management, and personal growth. Most people have taken a course on individual or team development — yet according to a recent poll, only a few have participated in any kind of program to develop one-on-one relationships.

TOO MUCH FOCUS ON *ME*?

Friendships add significant value to our marriages, families, work, and lives. At some level, everything we see and feel is the product of a personal relationship. Look around you and see if you can identify anything created in true isolation. After pondering this for a few moments, you might notice how dependent we are on connections with other people. Remove relationships from the equation, and everything disappears.

Yet when we think consciously about improving our lives, we focus our development inward. We strive to be better human beings. We try to make ourselves better employees. Even when we step back and focus on developing another person, as great parents and managers do so well, most of our emphasis is on the other person as an *individual*. We simply bypass the relationship itself.

As a result, millions are flat-out disengaged in their marriages and other close friendships. Why does this happen? Perhaps this situation evolved as a product of the "focus on me" environment. The majority of courses, professional development programs, and books highlight how to improve *yourself*. You take courses in grade school to improve *your own* ability to read, write, add, and subtract. Then as you progress through the educational system, you have the opportunity to spend more time educating *yourself* in areas *you* choose. When you enter the workforce, you might get the chance to add to *your* base of knowledge by participating in training and development programs designed to make you a better *individual* employee.

Educating oneself is the foundation of our learning systems, and it's obviously a worthwhile pursuit. But is there any chance it's time to add the next element? Have you ever taken a course in friendships? Could a second-grade student, a high-school junior, a college freshman, your boss, or even you benefit from time dedicated to this pursuit? If we have already spent significant time on self-development, is it possible that most of the magic — our room for rapid personal and professional growth — lies in developing our friendships?

Perhaps focusing on the *individual* is too narrow — and focusing on the *entire group* is too broad. The real energy occurs in each connection *between two people*, which can bring about exponential returns.

A MONUMENTAL CHALLENGE

In the 1940s, a connection between two historical giants forever altered our world. Although U.S. President Franklin Delano Roosevelt and British Prime Minister Winston Churchill had met years before, their relationship quickly intensified in late 1942, following the United States' entry into World War II. As their respective nations joined in battle, Roosevelt and Churchill spent several days together in Washington, D.C. During this time, as Jon Meacham eloquently describes in his book *Franklin and Winston: An Intimate Portrait of an Epic Friendship*, they would stay up until 2:00 in the morning having drinks and cigars and discussing the war, domestic politics, and their families. They got to know one another on a deeply personal level. This set the stage for a friendship that the world desperately needed in early 1943.

At the height of the war, Roosevelt and Churchill met in secluded locations. During one retreat, they drove together from Casablanca to Marrakech — even stopping along the way to have a picnic lunch. As the president was leaving Marrakech, Churchill told an aide he did not want to know when Roosevelt's plane left the ground (it was the first transatlantic flight by a U.S. president), saying, "It makes me far too nervous. If anything happened to that man, I couldn't stand it. He is the truest friend; he has the farthest vision; he is the greatest man I've ever known."

Like any friendship, theirs was not all roses. Roosevelt and Churchill knew one another's strengths and flaws, and at times, they made fairly cutting remarks and were critical of each other. But overall, it was clear that a strong bond existed — one that extended beyond the world stage. In one sentimental note, Churchill wrote to Roosevelt and said, "Our friendship is the rock on which I build for the future of the world so long as I am one of the builders."

Throughout World War II, Roosevelt and Churchill exchanged nearly 2,000 letters; spent more than a hundred days together; and celebrated Thanksgiving, Christmas, and New Year's Day with each other. Perhaps most importantly, by mid-1944, a product of this relationship, the allied coalition, was clearly winning the war. These two world powers and their respective leaders had been there for one another in times of dire need and were about to prevail.

In 1945, with the war drawing to a close and victory at hand, an ailing Roosevelt turned his attention to the future. On April 11, the day before he died, Roosevelt sat on the porch of his vacation home in Warm Springs, Georgia. As he penned a Jefferson

Day speech, the president contemplated society's next big challenge.

Roosevelt had already overcome paralysis, led the United States out of the Great Depression, and the allies were on the verge of winning World War II. Now, in the last 24 hours of his life, he peered into the future. With age-old walls crumbling around the globe and discrimination under fire at home, Roosevelt, perhaps inspired in part by his close bond with Churchill, found a common thread — one that could reconcile people around the world. Roosevelt would not live to deliver this speech, but his words offered a challenge for generations to come:

"Today we are faced with the pre-eminent fact that, if civilization is to survive, we must cultivate the science of human relationships."

CHAPTER 3:
BETTER THAN PROZAC?

Reading Franklin Roosevelt's prophetic words made me wonder: Have we learned much about the real *science* of relationships since his death in 1945? After reviewing a great deal of research on this topic, it turns out we have.

For starters, scientists have found that friends are catalysts for high points in any given day. They learned that even the dreaded commute to work is tolerable if it involves riding with a friend. The presence of a friend can make some of the most tedious activities enjoyable. Perhaps most importantly, strong social relationships are *the* leading indicator of our overall happiness, and these findings appear to hold up across countries and cultures.

A RAPID DECLINE

During our teenage years, we spend nearly one-third of our time with friends.

For the rest of our lives, the average time spent with friends is less than 10%.

Scientists are also uncovering how friendships shape our expectations, desires, and goals for the future. A 2003 study revealed how our closest relationships have a powerful effect on our behavior — even in the absence of the other person. It appears that close relationships can influence beliefs that endure for decades.

To examine how much friendships influence our long-held beliefs like religious preference, I surveyed more than 1,000 people on this topic. To my surprise, about 20% reported that their current religious preference was primarily shaped by their "own inquiry." Yet, later in this survey, I asked the same group about their parents' and best friend's religious preferences and found that fewer than 2% have a religious preference that differs from that of their best friend or a parent. Even though we think our choices are fairly independent, when you trace back to the origin of major beliefs, a close relationship is often sitting near the source.

YOU ARE WHO YOU EAT WITH

A colleague of mine, Rebecca, described how much her relationships have affected her diet and physical health. When she started dating a former competitive wrestler, her eating patterns quickly began to mirror his "extreme diet." Being a wrestler all his life, he was used to loading up on pizza, cheesesteaks, and milkshakes — and then going two days in a row without eating to take off the weight. Rebecca described how she would "eat the same junk he did" at mealtime, but then went back to her normal eating habits during his two-day starvation routine. Even though her boyfriend was able to maintain a normal weight on this not-so-healthy diet, Rebecca gained 15 pounds. "At the time," she said, "I never really thought about how much he influenced my diet."

Luckily, Rebecca's relationship with the former wrestler was short-lived, and soon thereafter, she started dating someone who was more health-conscious. Initially, it was hard for her to go back to a normal diet, but eventually she adjusted. Six months later, she was feeling better than ever, had more energy, was exercising regularly, and had lost 20 pounds.

After listening to Rebecca's testimony about the way her relationships had shaped her diet, I wanted to know if this was common. So I asked a group of 104 colleagues to respond to a brief questionnaire about their own diet and their best friend's diet. It turned out the two were even more closely intertwined than

I would have guessed. Those who reported having a best friend with a "very healthy" diet were more than five times as likely to have a very healthy diet themselves, when compared to people who had best friends with an average diet.

When I asked a similar question about "your best friend's level of physical activity," the results were just as striking. In fact, of the 104 people surveyed, among those who had a best friend who was *not* physically active, *not one* was very physically active themselves. A few months later, we asked a random sampling of 1,005 people the same questions about diet and exercise. We found similar results. Even if these findings are confounded by other variables, it appears that your best friend might just shape you in a more literal way than you ever imagined.

SHAPING YOUR WAISTLINE?

If your best friend has a very healthy diet, you are five times as likely to have a very healthy diet yourself.

THE FRIENDSHIP PRESCRIPTION

In addition to improving our health and life satisfaction, studies are now revealing how friends play a similar role during stressful times. Our friends essentially serve as a buffer during life challenges, which improves our cardiovascular functioning and resiliency and decreases our stress levels. When a tragic event occurs, a close friend becomes our comfort and refuge.

In a 2001 study, researchers at Duke University Medical Center explored the protective effect of friendships in more depth by studying patients with heart disease. They had already discovered that people with fewer than four friends were at a significant disadvantage. Over a four-year span, people in the "isolated" group (those with fewer than four friends) were *more than twice as likely to die* from heart disease. But the researchers wanted to know why. They suspected that several psychological and environmental factors led to the increase: stress, social status, income, smoking, hostility, or simply the severity of a patient's initial heart disease.

To the research team's surprise, based on a statistical analysis of 430 patients, *none* of these other factors accounted for the increased death rate among isolated patients. Even when they controlled for all of the aforementioned factors, the team found that having at least four friends helped people live significantly longer.

The more friends the better? Not necessarily. People in this study with five, six, seven, or eight friends gained about the same survival benefit, when compared to those with four friends. Having at least four friends appears to provide the maximum protective effect.

In summarizing the latest research from the Duke study and our own, it looks like we might not need an extraordinarily wide *breadth* of friends; it is likely to be the *quality* of our friendships that matters most. Each person needs a few very deep friendships to thrive. As you might suspect, lonely people suffer psychologically and physically. The absence of high-quality friendships is bad for our health, spirits, productivity, and longevity.

"Friendship has a profound effect on your physical well-being," writes Eugene Kennedy, Ph.D., professor of psychology at Loyola University of Chicago. "Having good relationships improves health and lifts depressions. You don't necessarily need drugs or medical treatment to accomplish this — just friends."

CHAPTER 4:
THE SILVER LINING
IN A MARRIAGE

"It is not a lack of love, but a lack of friendship that makes unhappy marriages."

— *Friedrich Nietzsche*

It would be hard to discuss friendships without talking about an intimate, loving relationship with a spouse or significant other, which, in many cases, is *the* most important friendship in a person's life. The topic of marriage is also pertinent because, whether we like it or not, marital satisfaction — or the lack of it — spills over into our work and all other areas of our lives. Marital satisfaction not only predicts happiness, according to our find-ings, but also workplace engagement. And if you are married, your satisfaction with life literally depends on the happiness of your spouse. As in any close relationship, one person's happiness or misery spreads to the other person quickly.

British economist Nick Powdthavee, who has developed complex formulas for quantifying the value of spousal relation-ships, discovered that a 30% increase in your spouse's happiness can have a tremendous effect. Powdthavee estimates that this in-crease can completely offset the emotional cost of losing your job or spending two months in the hospital.

On the other hand, negativity in a marriage has been shown to cause health problems. In fact, a 2005 study revealed how marital strife can delay the healing of physical wounds. To study the impact of arguments and stress on married couples, a group of Ohio State researchers recruited 42 couples, admitted them to the hospital, created eight small blisters on their arms, and then placed devices over the wounds that measured healing. The cou-ples also completed questionnaires and provided blood samples for analysis.

According to Professor Jan Kiecolt-Glaser, one of the lead investigators, "Wounds on the hostile couples healed at only 60 percent of the rate of couples considered to have low levels of hos-tility." So having an unhappy marriage could nearly *double* the time it takes for you to heal from an injury. In addition, blood samples from the more hostile couples contained 1.5 times the levels of interleukin-6 (IL-6) compared to the less hostile couples' samples. Sustained heightened levels of this protein in the bloodstream have been linked to increased risk for cardiovascular disease, osteoporosis, arthritis, Type 2 diabetes, Alzheimer's, and certain cancers, among other illnesses, according to the researchers. It appears that having a positive marriage profoundly influences our short-term and long-term physical health, from healing a blister to warding off cancer.

FOCUSING ON WHAT'S RIGHT

Unfortunately, current divorce rates suggest that too many marriages are mired in an unhealthy negativity. You have probably heard this alarming statistic before, but nearly half of all marriages end in divorce. What specifically leads couples to divorce versus staying together over time? According to Dr. John Gottman, one of the world's leading marriage researchers, the determining factor is *the quality of the couple's friendship*. In fact, Gallup's research indicates that a couple's friendship quality could account for 70% of overall marital satisfaction.

SEX OR FRIENDSHIP?

What drives marital satisfaction?
"The quality of a couple's friendship" is five times
as important as "physical intimacy."

Unlike other academics who prefer to stay in the lab, Gottman has conducted a great deal of work in the field to help improve marriage therapy techniques, hoping to decrease divorce rates. His workshops with hundreds of couples — in particular, couples at high risk for divorce — have been twice as effective as standard marital therapy.

What does Gottman do differently? "At the heart of my program is the simple truth that happy marriages are based on a deep friendship," he says. He helps couples focus on the smaller, day-to-day interactions that build a true, lasting friendship. Gottman advises couples to ask questions about what the other person is doing daily, to focus on helping with small but meaningful acts like doing the laundry, and to try and make the briefest of exchanges and subsequent memories more positive. This is what fuels romance and offers protection against adversarial situations.

Then why have so many other marriage therapists failed? According to Gottman: "Like so many experts before me, I was wrong. I was not able to crack the code to saving marriages until I started to analyze what went *right* in happy marriages." He discovered that most couples fight — but what differentiates happily married couples from the rest is the way they get along when they are *not* fighting. Based on my investigation, this holds true for almost any relationship. To judge a relationship based on its low points would be a mistake. The best gauge of a friendship's health is each person's happiness during everyday interactions.

CHAPTER 5:
THE ROUNDING ERROR

As a newlywed, Judy thought her marriage to Tim was headed in the right direction. They both had good jobs, a nice home in suburban Chicago, and they were sure their marriage would last forever. Friends viewed them as "the perfect couple," and they planned on living up to this expectation.

But as they neared their second anniversary, real doubt started creeping into Judy's mind. Frankly, she wasn't sure the marriage would last. Judy tried to pinpoint the problem, but she had no luck. Tim was still the same caring, handsome guy she had met four years earlier. She loved him deeply. And Tim wasn't doing anything wrong. He was always around, helped with things at home, and was exceptionally trustworthy.

So why was Judy always frustrated with Tim? When they sat down for dinner, Judy would start talking about her work. Tim listened well, but when she asked him for ideas and solutions to projects she was working on or people she was having trouble with, he didn't have much to offer. When she talked of going back to school to get a graduate degree, he was supportive, but he didn't necessarily encourage her.

Then Judy realized what the problem was. Throughout her life, Judy relied on other people to push her. Early on, her dad encouraged her, and more recently, her best friend from college, Lynn, always urged her to do more. Now that she was married, she didn't spend as much time with her dad or Lynn. So why wasn't Tim filling this gap? *What was his problem?* Judy wondered. She always pushed *him* to do more at work. In fact, Judy had recently prodded Tim to finish a standardized test he needed to complete to keep his career heading in the right direction. After he passed the test, Tim told Judy how much her encouragement helped. Didn't he owe it to her to do the same?

With this question fresh in her mind, Judy thought she had found the solution to getting her marriage back on track. She just needed to talk with Tim and help him understand how to meet her needs. The next night, as they were sitting on the couch having a glass of wine, Judy brought her concern to Tim's attention. Without being confrontational or accusatory, she explained what was happening and told him she needed more advice and "push." At first, Tim was a little defensive, but then he let his guard down and agreed to try.

For the next few months, Tim made several conscious efforts to encourage and challenge his wife. At first, it looked like his efforts might pay off. Judy could tell he was doing his best. But after a while, she realized Tim's best was equivalent to what her friend, Lynn, offered on a bad day. No matter how hard Tim tried, he was not a natural in this department. After all, this was the guy who hired a personal trainer so someone would force *him* to show up at the gym. In Judy's mind, things were taking another turn for the worse. Although she had yet to say this aloud, to Tim or anyone else, Judy once again started to ask herself if they were headed toward divorce.

THE MYTH OF WELL-ROUNDEDNESS

Problems like this occur all the time in marriages and very close friendships. We expect the other person to meet our every need — to be the one who pushes us to achieve; who listens unconditionally; who always lends a hand; and who is, all the while, the most fun. I have done this myself. Whether it was a good friend, someone I was dating, or a colleague at work, I always expected that person to do several different things to uphold his or her end of the relationship. But it never happened, and I was always disappointed.

Maybe I should have looked in the mirror. When thinking about my friendships — from the vantage point of the other person — it is clear that I cannot meet many of the expectations I have had of others. I am not the most patient person. As a fairly shy guy, I am not the friend who can help connect others to a broad social network. And I am not the laid-back type who can help others relax. Instead, I gravitate toward challenging my closest friends and giving them guidance.

There are countless things we expect from our friendships. You may have had a parent, teacher, or manager who expected you to be good at nearly everything. If so, you know how frustrating it can be when another person expects so much from you, and — no matter what you do — you cannot deliver. It is unlikely that one person can deliver everything, according to our research.

The problem is, friendships are not designed to be well-rounded; 83% of the people we have studied report that they bring different strengths to the relationship than their best friend does. This is why it's so damaging when another person focuses on what *we do not bring* to the friendship. According to our research, this negative focus:

- increases stress levels

- decreases marital satisfaction

- decreases satisfaction with friendships in general

Consequently, we should not expect *any* of our friends to be good at *everything*. This "rounding error" can poison the very best friendships and marriages.

RECIPROCAL, BUT NOT IN THE SAME WAYS

83% of people bring different strengths to the relationship than their best friend does.

ONE PERSON *CAN'T* DO IT ALL

After much agonizing over the subject, Judy accepted that Tim was not the best person for her to rely on for encouragement, and she began looking to other friends and colleagues when she needed to be challenged. Once Judy stopped "rounding" Tim, her marriage changed for the better. She started spending more time with her old friend Lynn, who always pushed her to achieve. Judy also realized that one of her coworkers was encouraging her whenever they worked on projects together, so she decided to spend more time building this workplace friendship.

Judy started to view her husband in a different light. She appreciated Tim's many good qualities even more. He knew her so well, and he could sense what she wanted even before she asked. He was the only person who had ever been in sync with her emotions in this way, and it meant the world to her. Whenever they spent time together — with friends or alone — he always made things fun. Tim had a knack for giving his friends a lift when they needed it.

A year later, looking back at the situation, Judy could hardly believe she had considered leaving her husband. He was, and had always been, the right man for her. Tim brought so much to their friendship: love, unconditional trust, humor, and much more. Judy felt foolish for fixating on the few things he *did not* bring to the relationship. In hindsight, it was all so straightforward and simple. After spending the last year focusing on what Tim *was* bringing to the friendship, their marriage was flourishing.

Judy had uncovered the key to any great friendship: focusing on what each friend *does* contribute to your life.

CHAPTER 6:
DOES WORK BALANCE LIFE?

"Balance is bunk! It's the central myth of the modern workplace:
With a few compromises, you can have it all. But it's all wrong,
and it's making us crazy."

— Fast Company *magazine*

The scenario that played out between Tim and Judy occurs in the workplace every day, albeit to a different degree. Most of us have dealt with a boss or colleague who commits the rounding error on a regular basis, and we know how that can set up the relationship for failure. Our latest research suggests that relationships at work and outside the office have a powerful influence on each other, so it's important to give more thought to our workplace relationships.

Consider what happens when you're getting ready to leave home in the morning and someone in your household is in a particularly foul mood. Chances are, this would bring you down too and would worsen your first few interactions with people at work.

Or let's say you're getting ready to leave work one day, and your boss walks in at the last minute. He drops in to tell you what a great job you had done on an important proposal. This gives you quite a lift and is a perfect way to end the day. As a result, you might have more positive exchanges with your friends or family members when you get home.

Conversely, if your boss had berated you and criticized the proposal, it probably would have cast a gloomy, oppressive shadow over your home that evening. A habitually negative colleague can have far-reaching effects that cascade from one person to the next.

Years ago, my friend Mark worked with a woman who managed to dampen her coworkers' spirits on a daily basis. This, in turn, led Mark to complain about "Sara" several times per week, which was frustrating for me. For a few months, this woman I had never met was doing more to detract from my happiness than anyone else in my life. And this was not an exception; apparently, several people where Mark worked were having trouble at home and were considering quitting because of Sara. One angry husband, whose pregnant wife worked with Sara, went as far as to call and tell her to leave his wife alone because he was concerned that all the stress was putting his wife's pregnancy in jeopardy. Unfortunately, Sara's boss continued to underestimate the impact of this negativity, and my friend Mark, along with many others, left the company soon thereafter.

A recent study revealed that employees definitely do bring negative moods home at night. "The boundaries between work and family are pretty permeable, and this is one more piece of evidence that people do tend to take their work home," says Tim Judge, a well-known management professor who led this research. Judge describes how employers "contribute to positive moods in both work and family life by the way they treat employees."

Everyone talks about the need for work/life balance — but it might not be that easy to separate the two. Your personal life doesn't stop when you get to work — and you don't stop thinking about work when you go home at night. Indeed, if work doesn't even enter your mind at night or on the weekends, this doesn't necessarily mean that you've attained the elusive work/life balance. It's more likely an indicator of how little you care about your job.

Balancing your time is one thing, but trying to create balance with relationships and emotions is very different. The data I have examined reveal a world of friendships that does not abide by the work/life balance credo. The emotional boundaries between work and personal life are blurred, and that might be a good thing. If you dread going home after work, things are clearly out of balance, and you might need to examine what's wrong with your relationships at home — and vice versa.

Perhaps balance is about having great friendships that extend between work and home. This is easier said than done, of course. While we spend more than half of our waking hours at work, most organizations have done very little to encourage friendships on the job. Some go as far as to prohibit close relationships, which could be a catastrophic mistake.

PART TWO: FRIENDS AT WORK

CHAPTER 7:
THE THREE-FRIEND THRESHOLD

These are the voices of people I have interviewed about workplace friendships:

"As a manager, I get concerned whenever my employees are fraternizing too much on the job."

"Close relationships on the job are messy. I like to keep my work and non-work life very separate from one another."

"I have plenty of friends, and I do not feel the need to get that close to people at work."

"We don't want people to have best friends at work."

Although some businesses are warming up to the idea of on-the-job friendships, there is still a strong resistance to them. Nearly one-third of the 80,000 managers and leaders we interviewed agreed with the statement "Familiarity breeds contempt." This probably doesn't come as a surprise to anyone who has ever worked in a large, bureaucratic organization.

NO FRIENDS ALLOWED

Laura learned the hard way just how much workplace friendships are discouraged when she went to work as a sales associate for one of the world's largest apparel retailers. Laura's manager, Beth, was one of her closest friends before they started working together. But Laura knew this had to remain a secret because her employer had a formal policy prohibiting managers and their employees from having friendships that extend beyond the workplace. Legend had it that one store manager was even disciplined for talking to an employee, in passing, at a local restaurant. Apparently, managers were not supposed to do anything other than say "hello" if they encountered a subordinate outside of work. So Beth and Laura were forced to conceal their friendship during business hours. But beyond that, they weren't afraid to socialize, primarily because they worked in a large city and never ran into coworkers when they were out together. The situation was not ideal, but it was bearable.

When Laura transferred to another store in a small community, however, a workplace friendship created much larger problems. Laura and her husband didn't have any friends or relatives in the area, and they both spent the majority of their time at work. Laura began to form a friendship with a shift supervisor, Yolanda. One morning when they were stocking the shelves, Yolanda invited Laura and another sales associate to join her for drinks after work. Laura assumed this wouldn't cause problems because Yolanda was a supervisor in another area and was not her manager. Besides, in a town this small, Laura felt she didn't have much choice if she wanted any social life. Laura eagerly accepted Yolanda's invitation.

They ended up having a great time, but unfortunately, they were spotted by another store employee who reported them to the company's 1-800 number that was dedicated to the anonymous reporting of violators. A few days later, the manager from a nearby store arrived and talked with Laura. According to Laura, "We got sat down. We were told that supervisors are not allowed to go out with people who aren't supervisors. You are not allowed to socialize in any aspect with someone who is not in your same position." Laura objected and explained her situation — that she was new to town — but she had no luck.

After these disciplinary talks, Laura and Yolanda were forced to discontinue their friendship to keep their jobs. Even though

Yolanda and another supervisor continued to socialize regularly after work, they never invited Laura again — "Just because I'm an associate," Laura explained. According to Laura, "Even though they know that I'm new in this town and don't have any other friends, they still would not do it."

Not only did this policy have an impact on Laura's friendship with Yolanda, but it caused her daily engagement on the job to plummet. The whole situation irreversibly changed the way Laura looked at her job. She said, "It makes it a lot less enjoyable of a workplace, knowing that you have to be very guarded about what you talk about, who you can be friends with, and what goes on outside of work."

Apparently, several major retailers post similar regulations in their stores and provide toll-free numbers for reporting violators. Such policies are more common than I had ever expected. Even if friendships are not actively discouraged, rarely does an organization's leadership encourage them.

LITTLE FOCUS ON
WORKPLACE FRIENDSHIPS

Only 18% of people work for organizations that provide opportunities to develop friendships on the job.

BELLYACHE BUDDIES

There are real risks when it comes to workplace friendships. A close friendship is inherently more complex than a superficial one. When people form tight-knit social groups at work, it can alienate others, who might become jealous and complain of cliques. And the closer two people get in the workplace, the more potential fallout if things go awry. The situation gets even more complicated when friendships turn romantic, especially if one party in the relationship is in a position of authority.

When interviewing former Detroit autoworkers, I observed several counterproductive workplace friendships. Within the typical auto factory, the relationship between management and union workers was so bad that it led to constant tension. As a result, most of the "friendships" between hourly workers were based on a mutual hatred for their employer. Whether employees were on the job or at the bar, their conversations usually revolved around complaining and venting.

Although this may be less common today, most workplaces have at least one pair of "bellyache buddies." So it's important to recognize the potentially negative consequences of some workplace friendships. However, according to recent research, the potential upside of friendships on the job could dramatically outweigh the possible disadvantages. New studies suggest that close friendships at work lead to substantial increases — not decreases — in job satisfaction and career success.

QUANTIFYING THE IMPACT

Curious about *how much* influence friendships can have in organizations, I assembled a diverse team of top researchers and thinkers from around the globe in 2004. Our goal was to examine the real financial and emotional impact of friendships on the job.

As much as I love numbers and statistics, I could easily spend a couple hundred pages discussing the findings from our research, but that would cause most of you to close this book for good. Instead, I will focus on the major discoveries of our study here. If you would like to learn more about the hundreds of questions we asked, the millions of interviews we analyzed, or other aspects of our research, please see Appendix D.

MAJOR DISCOVERIES FROM OUR RESEARCH

You might notice that we used the term "best friend" in our interviews. We did so because our early research indicated that having a "best friend" at work — rather than just a "friend" or even a "good friend" — was a more powerful predictor of workplace outcomes. Apparently, the word "friend" by itself has lost most of its exclusivity.

IF YOU HAVE A BEST FRIEND AT WORK, YOU ARE SIGNIFICANTLY MORE LIKELY TO:

- *engage your customers*

- *get more done in less time*

- *have fun on the job*

- *have a safe workplace with fewer accidents*

- *innovate and share new ideas*

- *feel informed and know that your opinions count*

- *have the opportunity to focus on your strengths each day*

Overall, *just 30%* of employees report having a best friend at work. If you are fortunate enough to be in this group, you are *seven times* as likely to be engaged in your job. Our results also suggest that people *without* a best friend at work all but eliminate their chances of being engaged during the workday.

Yet many organizations continue to discourage close relationships in the workplace. And as you can see from the highlights of our study, these organizations could be making a costly mistake. These studies indicate that the evolution and growth of friendships is a critical part of a healthy workplace. In the best workgroups we surveyed, employers recognize that people want to forge quality friendships and that company loyalty is built from such relationships.

Having friends at work might even form a type of emotional compensation for those who are lacking other incentives. Closer friendships at work can increase satisfaction with your company by nearly 50% — and can double the chances of having a favorable perception of your pay.

ABYSMAL ODDS

Without a best friend at work, the chances of being engaged in your job are 1 in 12.

IS ONE BEST FRIEND ENOUGH?

Most of the research I have mentioned is based on more than eight million responses to Gallup's "I have a best friend at work" survey item. Many companies are hesitant to ask employees if they have a best friend at work, yet it has consistently been one of the best predictors of an organization's profitability.

Given that we had already established the impact of having a best friend at work, I was curious to see if having additional close friends at work also made a difference. So, in a national study, we asked more than 1,000 people how many close friends they had. Next, each person was asked how many of those friends were also coworkers (this question was designed to get a more accurate response). At first, no significant differences emerged between those who have one versus two close friends at work. But the results for the group with at least three very close friendships showed another increase in work satisfaction and an even larger jump in life satisfaction. These data are far from conclusive, but it appears that three close friends may represent another major threshold.

THREE AT WORK, HAPPIER AT HOME?

People with at least three close friends at work were 96% more likely to be extremely satisfied with their life.

Don't get me wrong, having one best friend at work makes a world of difference. This is the first major step if you want a more enjoyable workplace and personal life. But don't stop when you have one great friend on the job. Based on the results of our latest research, you could see a dramatic difference if you build a few more friendships at work.

BUILDING LOYALTY *BETWEEN* EMPLOYEES

According to some research, we join and stay with groups, teams, and organizations because of our friends' involvement. This doesn't appear to change much over the course of our lives. In grade school, we join the same groups as our best friends. This continues through college and into the workplace. When we asked people if they would rather have a best friend at work or a 10% pay raise, having a friend clearly won.

As human beings, we want to take part in the same activities as our friends. Doing so makes us laugh and feel good, and it provides social support. And contrary to conventional wisdom, fears or tensions about friendships with coworkers of the opposite sex did not appear to be a major concern in our surveys; less than 10% of the people we studied are "very apprehensive" about close workplace relationships with someone of the opposite sex.

Think about the times when you have wanted to leave a group or organization. These are critical and defining moments, and having just one strong friend can make all the difference.

One woman I interviewed described how a friend at work had been the "glue" that kept her from leaving her job. Rosa, an executive for a large non-profit group, believed in her organization's mission. She had worked there for more than a decade, still enjoyed her job, and had a few close friends at work. But she got to a point when she was no longer sure that was enough. Her organization was having difficulty with its budget and started cutting costs. And a few interpersonal conflicts were starting to cause discord. At the end of one particularly difficult week, in which she was feeling extremely underappreciated, Rosa went home, thinking, "I'm done." All day Saturday and Sunday, she mulled over quitting her job, frequently in tears. On Sunday, she began writing a letter of resignation.

While she was writing the letter, she received a call from her best friend at work, a fellow member of the executive team. He called to say, "I've been thinking about you. I know last week was tough, and I just wanted you to know it will get better. The company needs you, and what you do is really important. I don't want you to give up." When Rosa got off the phone, she tore up her letter of resignation, showed up Monday morning, and continued to work alongside her best friend for several more years.

AN UNCOMMON FOCUS

Only 20% of employees dedicate time to developing friendships on the job.

While most companies spend their time thinking about how to increase an employee's loyalty to their organization, our results suggest they might want to try a different approach: *fostering the kind of loyalty that is built between one employee and another.* This is what keeps people in their jobs — and it extends far beyond businesses. Within faith-based organizations, we have found that close friendships are one of the best predictors of attendance, retention, satisfaction, and strength of belief in a higher power. So it appears that faith-based groups, schools, non-profits, sports teams, and other organizations are in the business of cultivating friendships, whether they realize it or not.

CHAPTER 8:
CAN YOU BE FRIENDS WITH YOUR BOSS?

"Managers learn in business school that relationships are either up or down, but the most important relationships today are sideways. If there is one thing that most of the people I know in management have to learn, it is how to handle relationships where there is no authority and no orders."

— *Management guru Peter Drucker*

When compared to time spent with relatives, children, customers, colleagues, or bosses, time spent with friends is rated as being the most enjoyable, according to a recent study. On average, time spent with a friend ranks even higher than time spent with your spouse. How could that be? The Princeton researchers who conducted this study used a novel technique: Participants were asked to reconstruct their day, allowing researchers to pinpoint specific moments. Participants also reported their overall enjoyment at each *moment*. For example, if you were in the midst of rushing your daughter to school or changing your son's dirty diaper, you might have been asked to report how happy you were at that moment. In contrast, you might have been asked to recall a moment with a friend when you were relaxing or having a drink together.

Perhaps most concerning was the bottom of this "people we enjoy being with" list. Clients and customers were third from the bottom; coworkers were second to last, followed by bosses, who were dead last. *Interacting with the boss was also rated, on average, as being less enjoyable than cleaning the house.*

THE PERSON WE *LEAST* LIKE TO BE AROUND

*Fewer than 1 in 5 people consider
their boss to be a close friend.*

Undoubtedly, there are thousands of managers in the workplace who have no business bearing the responsibility for developing other people. Most of us have had a boss like this at one point or another. They make you miserable, less productive, and even diminish your physical health. But we have also found thousands of exceptional managers who have the opposite effect, and they have something in common: These great managers care about each of their employees as a real human being, not just a means to an end.

When I spoke with employees who reported to Sandra, one of the highest rated managers we have ever studied, what amazed me was the variety in their descriptions of what she did best. It sounded as if they were talking about different people. One of Sandra's employees who did not need or want to be micromanaged told me that Sandra was the first manager who had given him "room to roam." Sandra was there for him, but she never looked over his shoulder on a daily basis.

In direct contrast, another one of Sandra's employees described how much she appreciated the way her boss "stopped in all the time to see how I was doing." She said, "I loved having a boss who cared about my family and was interested in *me*." This enabled her to get more done on the job. Apparently, this employee wanted and received regular attention.

IT HELPS TO BE FRIENDS

*Employees who have a close friendship
with their manager are more than 2.5 times as likely
to be satisfied with their job.*

Herein lies one of the secrets we have learned from top managers (and from great teachers, for that matter): They get to know each person as an individual, and they tailor their management to each employee's preferences.

We want and need managers who care about our lives beyond the workplace. Gallup has asked more than eight million people to respond to the statement "My supervisor, or someone at work, seems to care about me as a person" and has found that people who agree with this statement:

- are more likely to stay with the organization

- have more engaged customers

- are more productive

If you're fortunate enough to have had a manager who treated you like a friend and cared about your personal life, you probably understand the difference this type of genuine friendship can make. The best managers in the world are not only experts in systems, processes, and technical competencies — they are experts in *your life*. And, because of this, they increase your engagement and productivity at work.

HAVING A QUARTERLY DISCUSSION WITH YOUR BOSS?

Just 17% of employees report that their manager has made "an investment in our relationship" in the past three months.

All employees deserve a manager whom they can truly call a friend, or at least a manager who cares about their general well-being. The bottom line is that we spend roughly 50% more time with our customers, coworkers, and bosses than we do with our friends, significant others, children, and other relatives *combined*. If you want to be happier and more engaged at work, consider developing a few strong friendships at the office, maybe even one with your boss.

CHAPTER 9:
GETTING ENGAGED AT WORK

"Best friendships are good for business. Companies are coming to discover that, yet are at a loss at what to do about it."

— USA Today

Whenever I recommend that employees should have a "best friend at work," someone inevitably asks, "Great, but what can I do about it in my organization?" Leaders often view our research findings as a "nice to know" but don't see how they can be applied. In a recent newspaper interview, a senior executive with a well-known consulting firm acknowledged the importance of friendships at work but said, "We don't feel it is actionable."

One executive told me, "I can't just tell my people to make best friends." And another sarcastically commented, "Should I force them to go out and grab a beer together?" They're right; these approaches would not work.

But our research shows that employees *can* build best friendships on the job. In every organization and industry we study, scores on our "I have a best friend at work" item can increase with a little effort. And when they do, bottom-line results are likely to follow.

A QUICK WAY TO CREATE FRIENDSHIPS?

When managers discuss friendships with employees on a regular basis, it nearly triples the chances of employees having a "best friend at work."

CAN THE "OLD BLOKES" BECOME BEST FRIENDS?

In 2004, I attended a global conference that was hosted by one of the world's largest manufacturing companies. The night before the conference, I met Carolyn, a plant manager from Manchester, England. Carolyn was scheduled to make a presentation to the entire group — hundreds of managers and leaders from around the world — the next morning. She was very candid with me about how nervous she was. Carolyn had been asked to give a talk because of her plant's superior performance, but she had almost no experience with public speaking.

The next morning, I took a seat in the back row. As Carolyn was introduced to the group, I found myself vicariously nervous. Here she was, presenting to a group of senior executives from around the world, and her task was to help them understand *her* approach to engaging employees and building a better manufacturing plant . . . not an easy assignment.

Carolyn's fair skin turned a few shades of red as she started talking, but once she settled into her natural, conversational style, the audience tuned in quickly. She described the situation four years prior, when her plant measured employee engagement levels for the first time. Carolyn's group had some of the lowest scores in the company. Their safety record wasn't good, absences were high, customer complaints were soaring, and overall performance numbers were suffering. When things didn't get better the second year, someone from corporate called Carolyn and suggested that she devote more attention to improving employee engagement. If she did, the executives suggested to Carolyn, her key outcomes and metrics should improve.

When Carolyn looked at the questions used to measure employee engagement, she noticed that a couple of the items seemed "soft," especially for her environment. Carolyn was a rarity — a young female managing a plant where every employee on the line was a man, and most of them were over 40. The last thing she wanted to do was sit down with these "old blokes," as she called them, and talk about increasing scores on a question like "I have a best friend at work." But things were clearly getting worse, and she was desperate. She wasn't convinced it would help much, but she decided to give it a shot.

Over the next year, Carolyn recounted, she did everything she could to engage her employees on a more emotional level. At first, she said, the men thought she was a bit crazy — the way she talked about how they should care for each other and develop friendships. Carolyn persisted, spending more time talking with the guys on the floor and setting up opportunities for them to form closer relationships. She established a social fund that gave employees money for outings with their coworkers and family members. Carolyn said she focused on the "simple stuff" and tried to keep a constant flow of communication moving throughout the plant. She explained, "You know, people don't always hear what they want to, but they appreciate hearing something."

After a few months, she could see things changing at the plant. The men were having more casual conversations, and a few even looked like they were enjoying their jobs. In addition to going to the pub together after work, they went cycling and played badminton, football, and cards in large groups. Perhaps most importantly, "They do an awful lot of big things to help support each other," Carolyn said.

When one man was having trouble in his marriage, his work team rallied around him in support and even brought the situation to Carolyn's attention so she could be sensitive to it. When someone was sick, others were quick to pick up the slack and work extra hours. The men had formed close friendships. Carolyn was cautiously optimistic as she awaited the results of her next employee engagement survey. She told our group, "I guess it would have been hard to get much worse."

It was time for us to see the results. Carolyn displayed the numbers: Her group's employee engagement had increased dramatically. And the team's performance, as measured by "line speed," or the average number of units produced in a day, was increasing rapidly as well. The plant's customer complaints were down 50% from the previous year. The audience was amazed by her results; you could hear a collective gasp as Carolyn's peers studied the slide.

Carolyn told us that after she saw the initial results, she became convinced "this soft stuff was working." The next year, she put even more time and effort into driving engagement among her employees. What's more, her employees finally started to buy in, which made Carolyn's job easier. The guys were having more fun and getting more done.

And the plant was becoming a safer place to work; when things went wrong on the assembly line, friends were much more likely to jump in and help their buddies. "The place looks brighter. It looks cleaner. People just seem to take more care around the work area," Carolyn explained. Later, she told me how she could now "come in to work on a dreary Monday morning and always hear a laugh." She said, "It's a hard thing to explain because it's something you really do *feel*."

Carolyn could tell the plant was a very different place to work than it was just two years before, so she expected her scores to increase again the next year. Not only did Carolyn's employee engagement scores rise again, her group set all-time records for average line speed — one of the most important measures in a manufacturing plant. They were now among the most engaged workgroups worldwide, their customer complaints were down by *another* 50%, and their absences were less than one-third of the industry average — an unlikely turnaround, to say the least.

Most importantly, Carolyn's customers could see the turnaround for themselves. One of her most dissatisfied customers from years past, upon touring the plant, described how he could "see and feel" the improvement on the line operators' faces. This had Carolyn beaming with pride.

As Carolyn finished her presentation, she was so at ease. It sounded as if she were telling her story to an old friend while sitting at a pub in Manchester. Before receiving a roaring standing ovation from her peers at the global conference, Carolyn concluded with a challenge to the group: "If it worked with these old blokes, it should work for anyone."

HOW FRIENDS SHAPE OUR WORK AND LIFE

As our research team studied thousands of workgroups like Carolyn's, we started to notice new patterns in the data. It was clear that friendships were vital to happiness and achievement on the job — yet we could also see that most individuals and organizations were falling short. So we decided to follow these patterns in the data, which were suggesting *how* different friendships shape our work and life.

PART THREE: DEVELOPING VITAL FRIENDSHIPS

CHAPTER 10:
SHARPENING EACH RELATIONSHIP

If you want to make a knife work more effectively, you sharpen the edge that is already designed to cut. Sharpening the opposite side of the blade would take a substantial amount of time and make the knife more dangerous. Attempting to sharpen the handle would simply defy common sense, as it was never meant to be sharpened. Yet as I mentioned in Chapter 5, this is what happens when "rounding" occurs in a friendship. We try and force one person to be sharp in every way — even when it's a useless or potentially destructive exercise.

Instead, the key is to know the areas where each friendship has the most potential for sharpening. The surveys we conducted revealed that people have significantly better friendships when they know and can easily describe *what each friend contributes* to the relationship. So instead of being content with these initial findings, our research team was eager to take things a step further.

The first obstacle we addressed was a basic but important one. Our vocabulary about friendships was unclear. As I mentioned before, the meaning of the word "friend" has lost some of its original intensity. You probably notice this in everyday interactions. A distant acquaintance might refer to you as her "good friend," or perhaps a business associate you have met just once refers to you as his friend. Needless to say, the word "friend" is not that exclusive anymore and borders on a generic label. This is why we started using the word "vital." It is a word that is not commonly used to describe friendships, and it means something that is essential to your life.

Vi•tal Friend (vīt"l frend) *n.* 1. someone who measurably improves your life. 2. a person at work or in your personal life whom you can't afford to live without.

We also agreed on a more objective litmus test for a vital friendship, using the following questions:

If this person were no longer around, would your overall satisfaction with life decrease?

If this person were no longer a part of your life, would your achievement or engagement at work decrease?

If you can answer yes to *either* or *both* of these questions, then you have found a vital friend.

UNIQUE CONTRIBUTIONS

As we asked people to describe *how* each friend improved their work and life, we did not discover a single prototype or ideal friend. Although some people wanted one friend to do everything, it was not happening. Instead, we heard people describe friends who were *very good* at a *few things*. This was the big "aha!" for our research team — it looked as if there were several vital roles that friends bring to our lives.

In order to measure and describe the unique roles that friends play, we decided to create an assessment. To construct this assessment, we began by exploring the basic needs friends meet in our lives. We tested hundreds of ideas and questions, eventually identifying 66 items and eight Vital Roles (each role will be described in more detail in the next chapter) that differentiated positive and productive friendships from the rest.

We arrived at these eight Vital Roles by asking people about the things they are *getting* from their friendship with another person. In other words, I am qualified to say that my friend Mark is always there for me in my times of need. I know he plays that role in my life. But I am not the most qualified person to say that I am always there for Mark in *his* times of need. Mark would be the best person to answer that question.

As a result, the Vital Friends Assessment we developed focuses solely on the Vital Roles other people play in your life — what you are receiving from each friendship. It measures the strong points within your friendships but only tells one side of the story. Initially, it will reveal what you're getting, not what you're giving.

This is an important distinction because in a friendship, *we usually give different things than we receive*. Vital friendship roles are not always reciprocated — nor do they need to be. You might contribute guidance and motivation to a friendship, while the other person does not. But the other person might add a great deal to your life because he or she has many of the same interests you do, and you have fun when you spend time together. In some relationships, you and your friend will play the same roles for one another — but that is not the norm.

THE NEED FOR A COMMON LANGUAGE?

*Only 30% of people find it easy to describe what
each friend contributes to their life.*

This is why it's ideal if both friends in a relationship participate in the Vital Friends Assessment and have a discussion about the results. This will allow you to see the Vital Roles you play in each other's lives. Above all else, we want this assessment to provide a language for talking about what is working in your friendships.

WHAT ROLES DO EACH OF YOUR FRIENDS PLAY?

The Vital Friends Assessment was designed to measure the eight most common friendship roles that we identified in our research. However, it will *not* capture *every* dimension and nuance of your friendships. By no means is this a complete or perfect list. There are hundreds of unique roles people play in your life. You will have friends who play specific roles in your life that are not included in this assessment. They certainly deserve your attention. I encourage you to add to this language liberally as you begin to study your friendships.

You may find that taking the Vital Friends Assessment in and of itself is interesting, but it *alone* will not lead to lasting growth. This assessment is just a starting point to help you identify what is right with your relationships. The next step is finding unique ways to build and extend these connections. That is the ultimate destination.

In conjunction with this book, you will be able to create your own customized Vital Friends website. You start by entering a friend's name, and then you complete a short survey (the Vital Friends Assessment) with that person in mind. When you take the survey, your friend's name will appear in the questions. For example, if you enter the name "Julie," an item will read: *"Julie can anticipate my next move."*

The assessment will take about five minutes per friend. Upon completion of each assessment, you will receive a report that lists the top three Vital Roles your friend plays in your life in descending order of intensity, based on your responses to the assessment. The key is to devote your attention to the roles this person *does* play in your life; this is where the opportunity for true growth lies.

The number of Vital Roles each friend contributes will vary from person to person. One extraordinary vital friendship can be many times more important than a handful of casual relationships. Some friends will play a few roles, while others will play a single role. Don't underestimate the friends who play just one role with excellence; this could have a powerful influence on your work and personal life. When you receive the Vital Friends report for each person, review it carefully and decide which roles are present in your friendship and which ones are not.

If a friend plays just one of the three Vital Roles, based on your own judgment, you can share that role with your friend and focus your attention in that direction. If you want to share all three roles with someone, I encourage you to do so. There is a feature on the website that allows you to choose the roles you want to share and then e-mail them to each friend. If a specific Vital Role does not appear in a close friend's top-three listing, but you know that it is present in the friendship, go ahead and claim it as a Vital Role — it might be hiding at #4. What's important is that you share this information right away to get the dialogue started.

After you complete the assessment for each of your friendships, refer to Chapter 11. It includes a reference section for each of the eight Vital Roles. This section provides a description of each role, a few real-life examples of how it plays out in friendships, and action items for building stronger friendships within the role. You will also find suggestions that apply if *you play this role for another person.* The descriptions, examples, and action items in this section were developed based on thousands of interviews with people who completed the assessment and described each Vital Role in detail. As a result, some of the descriptions and examples might fit your friendship better than others, so go ahead and choose the ones that describe each friendship best.

The Vital Friends website is also designed to help you catalog your vital friendships, and it can be used for developing stronger relationships. You might want to start with a few of your closest friends or colleagues, and then complete the assessment for other friends — or new friends — later. When you log on to the site, you will have a "Friends" page that lists all of the friends you have entered. You can watch as your network of friends grows or simply ensure that someone is playing each of the eight Vital Roles for you.

ACCESSING THE VITAL FRIENDS WEBSITE

1. Go to: www.vitalfriends.com.

2. Click on the "Sign In" button.

3. The first time you visit the site, you will need to register and create your account. To do this, you need your unique Vital Friends ID code, which can be found on the reverse side of the jacket of this book. During registration, you will create a user name and password.

4. Once you are registered, you can take the Vital Friends Assessment and customize your own website and Friends pages. On future visits to www.vitalfriends.com, sign in using your user name and password. You will then have access your personalized website and Friends pages.

CHAPTER 11:
THE EIGHT VITAL ROLES

BUILDER

CHAMPION

COLLABORATOR

COMPANION

CONNECTOR

ENERGIZER

MIND OPENER

NAVIGATOR

BUILDER

Builders are great motivators, always pushing you toward the finish line. They continually invest in your development and genuinely want you to succeed — even if it means they have to go out on a limb for you. Builders are generous with their time as they help you see your strengths and use them productively. When you want to think about how you can do more of what you already do well, talk to a Builder. Much like the best coaches and managers, these are the friends who lead you to achieve more each day. And great Builders will not compete with you. They figure out how their talents can complement yours. If you need a catalyst for your personal or professional growth, stay close to a Builder.

BUILDERS IN ACTION:

- *"Even though I had a successful business career, I never received a college degree. My friend George knew that this was an issue for me and that it made me feel inferior to some of our colleagues, clients, and even some of the people who report to me. He really encouraged me to go back to school and get my degree. Because of his encouragement and persistent support, I took the plunge, and now I have a bachelor's degree in business administration. I feel much more confident."*

  — Brad P., client services manager

- *"I started at a new company a year ago and really con-nected with my boss Spencer immediately. He has taken the time to make sure I am successful in my job through train-ing, meaningful conversations, and sharing of himself. He has invested a lot of time in me, which increases my level of confidence as I do my job. I like to work hard, but Spencer motivates me to work even harder because I know that his reputation is intertwined with my success, and I don't want to let him down."*

  — Macon C., recruitment specialist

- *"My manager Susan is a Builder for me. She praises me when I do good work, and she is always pushing me to do more. Last month, she asked me to create our annual re-port. I had worked on smaller pieces before, but never any-thing of this scale. I was nervous at first, but Susan gave me ideas, resources, and had faith in me. The final product exceeded everyone's expectations. Susan knew I could do it — when I didn't even know myself!"*

  — Steve B., public relations assistant

- *"I am in charge of the service side of a car dealership that my husband and I own. I wanted to get a better price on warranty service reimbursement from the automaker, but the paperwork was a real bear. My husband was so sup-portive and really encouraged me through the process. If it*

*wasn't for his confidence in my ability to complete the proj-
ect, I would have never finished. The result is that the company is paying us $17 more per hour for warranty work,
which I can pass right along to my employees."*

— Kay S., auto dealership owner

WHO ARE YOUR BUILDERS?

_____

_____

_____

STRENGTHENING YOUR BUILDERS:

- Help your Builders understand exactly where and when
  you could use a little extra push. Discuss your goals together so they can continually help you attain them. Give
  them permission to push and encourage you when they
  see you waver.

- When seeking advice from a Builder, bring your strengths
  to the forefront of the discussion. Builders want to invest
  in what you do well and help you see opportunities that
  you might otherwise miss. Builders see the best in you
  even when you can't.

- Your Builders may or may not be good at connecting you with others, but they will likely be good coaches. Seek them out before important meetings, interviews, or presentations. They know what you do well and can provide moral support.

- Share your successes with your Builders, and be sure they know how they helped you get there. Builders thrive on the intrinsic satisfaction they receive from your development — make sure to tell them about it.

CREATING NEW BUILDERS IN YOUR LIFE:

- Don't be shy about asking people for day-to-day advice, whether it is someone in a leadership role, a family member, or a coworker. People love to give advice. Asking for their advice will show them that you respect their insight. And, in the future, they might be more likely to take an interest in your development.

- Get to know people who seem to care about the success of others. They might have an innate desire to see others grow, and they could take an interest in your success.

- Share some personal information with potential Builders. The better people know you, the more they will understand your strengths and what makes you successful.

- If your supervisor doesn't play the role of Builder for you, perhaps it's because you haven't given him or her a chance. Make a quarterly appointment to touch base and discuss your successes and goals. If you let your supervisor know that this is important to you, he or she may take more of an interest in your success.

IF YOU ARE A BUILDER:

- Notice when your friends learn and grow. Enhance this growth by sharing your specific observations with them.

- Ask your friends about a success they recently had. Suggest what strengths you see in them that may have had a hand in their success. Be aware of opportunities that might help your friends succeed in the future, and bring them to your friends' attention.

- Make time to visit with your friends. Ask them to identify and discuss their strengths. Help them take pride in themselves by owning what makes them unique and special.

- Help your friends expand their ideas about what influences growth. Formal classroom learning is one way to grow, but diving in and offering to help with projects is another. The venues for growth and development are varied; consider work, school, and volunteer organizations.

- Think about ways that your friends' abilities complement yours. Figure out how you work best as a team.

- Talk to others about your friends and what they "bring to the table." Suggest areas in which you think your friends could really excel. Think about how you might help them succeed.

CHAMPION

Champions stand up for you and what you believe in. They are the friends who sing your praises. Every day, this makes a difference in your life. Not only do they praise you in your presence, a Champion also "has your back" — and will stand up for you when you're not around. They accept you for the person you are, even in the face of resistance. Champions are loyal friends with whom you can share things in confidence. They have a low tolerance for dishonesty. You can count on them to accept what you say, without judging, even when others do not. Champions are your best advocates. When you succeed, they are proud of you, and they share it with others. Champions thrive on your accomplishments and happiness. When you need someone to promote your cause, look to a Champion.

CHAMPIONS IN ACTION:

- *"My friend and coworker Mike is always aware of my successes and freely tells others. We had a meeting recently, and I was being quiet about a big accomplishment of mine. Then Mike told the group what I had done. Everyone congratulated me on my work, and it felt great. I would have been uncomfortable bringing it up myself, so I was grateful that Mike did it for me."*

    — Sarah L., education coordinator

- *"I was having a hard time with a few of my employees. It seemed they didn't understand my role and therefore were creating rumors about my level of competence. They didn't know that I took work home every night and the extent of my responsibilities. Fortunately, a member of my staff who worked more closely with me stepped up in my defense. I had tried to do this myself in the past, but it was so much more effective coming from within the ranks."*

  — Rajinder S., IT director

- *"I was recently selected for a new position within my organization. My husband had some concerns because of potential longer hours, but he was supportive enough. I felt so good, though, when I overheard him telling his father and several of his friends about my new job and how proud he was of me."*

  — Staci K., non-profit director

- *"Travis has really helped me achieve success in my job. He put in a good word about me to another colleague and landed me a position on a lucrative client team. He's very respected in the company, and so him saying good things about me really gives me that extra credibility. It's nice to have someone lobbying for me."*

  — Dee M., consultant

WHO ARE YOUR CHAMPIONS?

_____

_____

_____

STRENGTHENING YOUR CHAMPIONS:

- Help your Champions understand that their role may be like that of a celebrity's agent or a politician's campaign manager. Tell your Champions precisely what you want them to communicate to others about your abilities, interests, successes, goals, and aspirations.

- Let your Champions know when their kind words, comments, and compliments find their way back to you.

- Tell your Champions that you trust them and feel comfortable sharing your successes with them. Explain that it is not as easy for you to talk about your accomplishments with other people and that you are grateful for their support.

- When you make a mistake, share the problem with your Champions. You can expect honesty and nonjudgmental support from them.

CREATING NEW CHAMPIONS IN YOUR LIFE:

- Notice people who are always standing up for others. Get to know them, and build a relationship by thinking of ways you could become friends with them.

- Confide in potential Champion friends. Don't tell them your life story and unload your problems on them, but slowly let them know some of your dreams and fears.

- Quietly let others know about your accomplishments. Champions are more likely to surface and befriend you if they sense a certain humbleness. If you are busy boasting about your accomplishments, others might not feel that urge.

- While working on a project or special task, get buy-in from those around you. Ask for their opinions throughout the project — and when you are finished, let them know how much you appreciate them. If they feel they have contributed to your work and are just as proud of your accomplishments as you are, they will be inclined to share your success with others.

IF YOU ARE A CHAMPION:

- Ask your friends about their accomplishments. Stay up-to-date with what they've learned and achieved. They will love to tell you, and you will be able to help them — and others — see where their growth might take them in the future.

- Consider your spheres of influence. Perhaps you frequently advocate for your friends in the work environment. Are there other arenas where their talents might shine? Teaching, coaching, mentoring, and volunteering are needs in many venues — schools, clubs, sports, and faith communities. Expand your thinking about where you promote your friends.

- Check in regularly with your friends and ask what successes they have had at work or at home. You may have to probe a bit if they are reluctant to share. Have some questions prepared ahead of time to ask them.

- Ask your friends what they need from you to help set them up for success. Challenge yourself to provide it for them.

- Understand that your friends value your loyalty and may share things with you that they don't share with others. Honor that trust by keeping their confidence.

- Notice when your friends have successes, and congratulate them with notes or words of praise. Copy other friends or colleagues when you send them e-mails in which you praise them or thank them for their ideas, hard work, accomplishments, or suggestions. Remember to speak highly of your friends to the significant people in their personal lives. This includes their parents, spouses, children, and close friends.

COLLABORATOR

A Collaborator is a friend with similar interests — the basis for many great friendships. You might share a passion for sports, hobbies, religion, work, politics, food, music, movies, or books. In many cases, you belong to the same groups or share affiliations. When you talk with a Collaborator, you're on familiar ground, and this can serve as the foundation for a lasting relationship. Indeed, in those conversations, you often find that you have similar ambitions in work and life. Looking for someone who can relate to your passions? Find a Collaborator.

COLLABORATORS IN ACTION:

- *"My friend Dave and I went to college together, and socially, he's one of my best friends. We play golf and have been in a club together, in one form or another, for the last 20 years. There's a great depth to our friendship because of our shared experiences. I can't imagine life without him."*

  — Tony Y., chief financial officer

- *"Ten years ago, I met Molly at a community function. We shared a deep passion for helping underprivileged children in the community. Every few months, we would bump into each other and talk for a while. Eventually, we started volunteering at the same times. For the last five years, Molly has been my best friend."*

  — Carol C., community volunteer

- *"I have a corporate office job. In our spare time, my good friend Joe and I get together and brainstorm ways to improve the world. We started a group to encourage young people to vote in our community. This stemmed from our passion for the same thing — the way we see the world and our desire to make things happen. He is a kindred spirit. We wouldn't have accomplished nearly as much by ourselves as we have together."*

  — Jason L., human resources specialist

- *"I work at an animal shelter. Though our staff and volunteers are an eclectic mix, we all have one thing in common: We love animals. This commonality keeps us motivated to do our jobs, work together, and get to know each other better. It means a lot to me to work in a place where everyone shares a common interest."*

  — David C., operations manager

WHO ARE YOUR COLLABORATORS?

_____

_____

_____

STRENGTHENING YOUR COLLABORATORS:

- Send your Collaborators books or articles that would interest you both. Then, call your Collaborators to discuss these topics. This will give you even more of an anchor to deepen shared interests.

- Brainstorm ways to spend time with your Collaborator participating in a hobby you both enjoy. Perhaps the two of you could form a group at work, in your neighborhood, or at church based on your interests. For example, if you both like basketball, organize a basketball tournament. If you both enjoy movies, plan a get-together during the Academy Awards.

- Be aware of new opportunities that might interest your friends. Share this information with them on a regular basis.

- Acknowledge that while you may only get together occasionally to discuss a shared subject, you appreciate having someone in your life who shares the same passion. Tell your Collaborators that you think of them whenever that topic arises.

CREATING NEW COLLABORATORS IN YOUR LIFE:

- Let coworkers know about your interests and hobbies outside of work. Display things that are symbolic of your hobby or special interest in your home or office to attract like-minded enthusiasts. If you find someone with a similar hobby, your relationship will grow.

- Attend events, lectures, forums, or gatherings that interest you. Keep your eyes open for other attendees whom you know as acquaintances. Make an effort to reach out to them at the gathering, or make plans with them to discuss your common interests.

- Make a list of your interests, hobbies, and passions. Identify friends who share these interests, and use this as a guide for building new friendships.

- Volunteer for a club or organization with a mission or purpose you strongly believe in. Search the Internet or local resources for opportunities in your community to participate in meetings or activities these organizations have. You will find potential friends who are looking to meet people with a similar passion.

IF YOU ARE A COLLABORATOR:

- Make time to share stories and reminisce. Sharing stories and experiences strengthens common ground. Don't be shy about retelling a story — this can be a source of joy and fun.

- Surprise your friends with things that you know would interest them — a piece of information, a recipe, or tickets to a play. Others might not see their interests as clearly as you do.

- Think of ways to create traditions with your friend based on your shared interest. For example, if you both like baseball, make plans to go to the home opener together each year. If you both enjoy golf, make it a tradition to take the day off and play a few rounds on the first spring day every year. This tradition will give you something to look forward to and create good memories and stories to share.

- Invite others who have similar interests to join you in activities. Having shared friends will give you even more to discuss.

- Schedule a regular day to eat lunch or dinner together. Take turns selecting the restaurant or the meal. Planning this time together will help strengthen your relationship.

COMPANION

A Companion is always there for you, whatever the circumstances. You share a bond that is virtually unbreakable. When something big happens in your life — good or bad — this is one of the first people you call. At times, a true Companion will even sense where you are headed — your thoughts, feelings, and actions — before you know it yourself. Companions take pride in your relationship, and they will sacrifice for your benefit. They are the friends for whom you might literally put your life on the line. If you are searching for a friendship that can last a lifetime, look no further than a Companion.

COMPANIONS IN ACTION:

- *"Luke and I are partners in a restaurant business. We started out as salesmen for a restaurant company 20 years ago. One day, we played hooky and went fishing. That day, we decided to go into business for ourselves, and we have worked together ever since. I trust Luke with my life. There is nothing we wouldn't do for each other. He is like a brother to me."*

  — John C., business owner

- *"It is very hard to win my trust. I expect a lot from myself and those around me. When I find someone I can trust, I know they will be a lifelong friend. My friend and coworker*

Willy is an example of this. If he asks me to do something, I will do it — no questions asked. That's how much I trust him. Because of this, I love working on project teams with Willy."

— Joseph R., project engineer

- *"My wife is one in a million. We have been married for 35 years, and we know everything about each other. I love my job and other friends in my life, but at the end of the day, I feel so lucky to be able to go home to my best friend."*

  — Michael J., vice president of sales

- *"My friend Ben is someone I have known since second grade. He knows me better than anyone except my wife, and in some ways, he knows me better than my wife. He is someone I want to share significant things with immediately — both good and bad. It's a nice feeling to have someone with whom I can be so completely honest and let my guard down. I know he feels the same about me."*

  — John W., trust officer

WHO ARE YOUR COMPANIONS?

_____

_____

_____

STRENGTHENING YOUR COMPANIONS:

- With a Companion, you are safe to go beyond mundane, everyday events and talk about what matters most in life. Ask questions: "How have you changed? How have you grown? What do you fear? What do you want for your future?" Take time to open up so you stay connected at a deep level.

- Try to make an appointment once a month with your Companion to do something the two of you like to do. The best way to foster a Companion relationship is by spending quality time together.

- Surprise your Companions with special gifts that fit their personalities and show how you understand them. Consider writing a note or card to your Companions telling them how you feel about them and what they mean to you.

- Create a safe environment for your Companions to be themselves and share more of who they are. Remember to share the good news, as well as the bad, with your Companions. The highs will be even higher with these people. The lows will not seem as overwhelming when the burden is shared.

CREATING NEW COMPANIONS IN YOUR LIFE:

- Relationships develop through shared experiences, trust, and a deep bond. Look to your current friends to see which relationships can be strengthened and taken to a deeper level.

- If it is hard for you to open up to people, practice by sharing smaller things and letting your friends know that it is not easy for you to be vulnerable. This is a small but significant step toward building a deeper relationship.

- Remember that a Companion is often a mutual role — you are more likely to find a Companion in someone who sees you in the same light. Practice being a good listener, and allow potential Companions to be themselves.

- Spend time getting to know your parents, grandparents, siblings, or extended family better. The old axiom "You can't pick your relatives" may be true, but you also have some shared history and a bond that should not be taken for granted. Think of a favorite relative you have always liked but don't know that well. This person could have the potential to be a true Companion for you.

IF YOU ARE A COMPANION:

- When your friends are going through a hard time, be there for them. They will count on your friendship to strengthen them.

- Try not to keep secrets from your friends. Secrets will erode the trust between you.

- Create a safe environment for your friends. Seek to boost their spirits through compassion and understanding. Your friends care about you a great deal. It is important to treat them with dignity and respect.

- Work through any conflicts you may have with your friends as quickly as possible. Your good friends are such an integral part of your life that any issues with them will spill over into other areas.

- Tell your friends how much they mean to you. Because of your strong connection, you might not always remember to tell them how you feel about them.

- Do something special together to honor the bonds you have. In a busy or hectic life, it is sometimes easy to take the ones closest to us for granted. A gift or something special from you will mean a lot to them, so make it meaningful.

CONNECTOR*

A Connector is a bridge builder who helps you get what you want. Connectors get to know you — and then introduce you to others. These are the people you socialize with regularly. Friends who play the role of a Connector are always inviting you to lunch, dinner, drinks, and other gatherings where you can meet new people. This extends your network dramatically and gives you access to newfound resources. When you need something — a job, a doctor, a friend, or a date — a Connector points you in the right direction. They seem to "know everyone." If you need to get out more or simply want to widen your circle of friends or business associates, a Connector can help.

CONNECTORS IN ACTION:

- *"When I started at my company, I didn't know anyone. Then, in my second week, I met Leigh. She took me around and introduced me to everyone. This made my job a lot easier."*

  — Crystal K., project manager

- *"My business partner's mind is like a database of people. It's amazing because she knows so much about them too. She introduces people based on what they have in common. I think she wants to get to know people better — just so she can bring them into her network. This helps me meet new people every time I am at an event with her."*

  — Michelle M., attorney

* This term was originally described by Malcolm Gladwell in *The Tipping Point* (2000).

- *"My wife plays the role of Connector for me. I didn't realize how much because I think of Connectors as people in business relationships. But she runs my social life on the weekends. Some of the women she gets to know have husbands that I get to know. Her best friend's husband was an executive at a bank that happened to be one of my largest accounts. This connection has really helped strengthen the relationship with this client, and I made a new friend."*

  — Warren W., sales manager

- *"I tend to be very introverted and don't always seek out interesting opportunities even though I love learning new things. My friend Robert must know this about me because it seems like he is always suggesting conferences or workshops I can attend to help me do my job better. In the end, I am always grateful for his suggestions because I have learned so much from participating."*

  — Dan F., financial analyst

WHO ARE YOUR CONNECTORS?

_____

_____

_____

STRENGTHENING YOUR CONNECTORS:

- If you are looking to fill a position or change jobs, tell the Connectors in your life. Many jobs are filled or obtained through connections. Help your Connectors know how fundamental and important they are to you as you work to build your social or business network. Connectors love to help establish links for people.

- Ask Connectors for advice about the best restaurants, hair salons, car dealers, or contractors. They will have answers and connect you with the right people. They might even be able to get you a good deal.

- Let Connectors know your interests and future plans. They will naturally look for ways to introduce you to people who could help you achieve your goals.

- Remember to thank your Connectors when their advocacy for you gets you an audience with someone you have wanted to meet, results in your being given an assignment you enjoy, or gains you entry into an organization you have yearned to join.

CREATING NEW CONNECTORS IN YOUR LIFE:

- If a friend invites you to an event where you will have the opportunity to meet new people, accept the invitation.

If he is a Connector, he will introduce you and make you feel comfortable.

- If you are new to a job or social situation, make it a point to get to know the people who seem to know everyone. They will enjoy meeting you and introducing you to others.

- If you are shy or reserved by nature, and you find yourself in charge of a social or business gathering where few people are well-acquainted, invite people who love meeting strangers. They will naturally work to build connections between people and put them at ease. And, your invitation will flatter them.

- If you are outgoing, seek out others who seem to know everyone, and invite them to networking or social events. They will enjoy being asked and will likely return the favor.

IF YOU ARE A CONNECTOR:

- Let friends know that they can use you as a resource to get to the right information or to the right people for the things they need. They may be reluctant to "impose," so take the first step to put their fear to rest.

- Invite your friends to social engagements, parties, or events that they might not typically attend. If your friends are going through a period of loneliness or isolation, be the person who helps them reach out to other people. They will appreciate your support.

- Think of people it would be advantageous for your friends to meet. Your contacts may help them advance their careers or make new friends.

- If your friends are new to a group or work situation, introduce them to people you know. They will appreciate it and feel more welcomed. When introducing your friends to new people, tell them the things they have in common. This will give them something to talk about. They might not see the connection as easily as you do.

- Include your friends' names, titles, addresses, e-mail addresses, and phone numbers in your electronic contact list or day planner. This makes it easy for you to share their information with your other associates, friends, and family members.

- Think about your entire network of friends. Are there two people in your broad network who should get to know each other? Host an event and invite both of these people. This is a two-way connection opportunity.

ENERGIZER

Energizers are your "fun friends" who always give you a boost. You have more positive moments when you are with these friends. Energizers are quick to pick you up when you're down — and can make a good day great. They are always saying and doing things that make you feel better. Energizers have a remarkable ability to figure out what gets you going. When you are around these friends, you smile a lot more. You are more likely to laugh in the presence of an Energizer. If you want to relax and have a good time or need to get out of a rut, call an Energizer.

ENERGIZERS IN ACTION:

- *"I have worked for a dentist named James for the past 10 years. He just lights up the room. A lot of people are afraid of the dentist, but James makes it a fun experience for everyone. The result is that my days are packed with laughter. He is just so funny, and I never know what he will come up with next. Sometimes I leave work and my sides hurt because I have been laughing so hard."*

  — Stephanie F., oral hygienist

- *"My coworker Julie and I have been friends for 20 years. When I am having a particularly stressful week, she will invite me to lunch. Though I usually feel too busy to take lunch and prefer to eat on the fly, this nudge reminds me that it is important to take the time to enjoy life. I always feel ready to take on the world after our lunches together. She is so much fun and always seems to be just what the doctor ordered!"*

— Ann O., manager

- *"Sometimes my job can be very tough. There are days when I just want to tear my hair out. Whenever I am feeling this way, I stop by Josh's office, and he inevitably cheers me up with some funny story or imitation he likes to do. He cracks me up. I always feel better after having a laugh with Josh."*

  — Brian J., news director

- *"Our receptionist seems to smile at everyone who comes in the door. You can just tell she loves her job. When I arrive at work, I am usually groggy and needing that first cup of coffee, but when I see Phyllis, I can't help but smile. This may seem like a small thing, but it makes a difference almost every day."*

  — Josephine R., editor

- *"I have moved around a lot in my life and have friends all over the country. Erin is one friend who especially energizes me. I don't see her very often, but when we do have a chance to get together, we always have fun. I look forward to it for months in advance. When I need to step away from my daily life, I call her for a good laugh as we remember old times together."*

  — Grace E., property manager

WHO ARE YOUR ENERGIZERS?

_____

_____

_____

STRENGTHENING YOUR ENERGIZERS:

- If you have Energizer friends whose stories always make you laugh, encourage them by reminiscing about some of their best stories and having them share the stories with other people.

- It can be easy to focus on the negative aspects of those who are closest to us. With Energizer friends, it is especially important to focus on the positive so that you fully enjoy their company and so they will want to continue to play this Energizer role in your life.

- When you are feeling down or going through a period of stress, Energizers will likely try to lift your spirits. Sit back and allow yourself to see the brighter side of the situation.

- Help your Energizers see how the small things they do, on a daily basis, accumulate and add to your overall happiness. Show them how their ability to boost the positive emotions in a room can transform a home, school, or workplace.

CREATING NEW ENERGIZERS IN YOUR LIFE:

- Energizers come in all shapes and sizes. Some are outgoing and "the life of the party," while others quietly energize you. Discover the people who give you energy, and spend time with them.

- If you are looking to create energizing relationships, start by allowing yourself to be energized. If a friend or coworker makes an effort to increase your positive emotions, honor that effort by laughing at a silly joke or giving a warm-hearted smile in return.

- Allow yourself to be drawn to people with positive energy. Notice the people in your life who make you smile, make you laugh, and generally lift your spirits. Make an effort to spend more time with them.

- Become an Energizer for others by allowing your sense of humor to shine through in all situations. If you are able to laugh at yourself and help others see the positive side, they will do the same in return.

IF YOU ARE AN ENERGIZER:

- Call or e-mail your friends with jokes or funny anecdotes that will make them laugh.

- Encourage your friends to see the things that are going well for them. You can help keep them focused on the positive.

- When you play the Energizer role, your friends see your energy as contagious. For them to "catch" what you have, they need to have contact with you. When are the best times for you to have that kind of contact with them? Is your energy more contagious first thing in the morning when you are fresh or at the end of the day when your work is done?

- Give your friends feedback when they need it. Because you have a positive influence on their lives, this feedback will be more welcomed from you than from others.

- Help your friends take a mini-vacation without leaving town. Invite them to a movie, lunch, or some other activity where you can unwind and enjoy life.

MIND OPENER

Mind Openers are the friends who expand your horizons and encourage you to embrace new ideas, opportunities, cultures, and people. They challenge you to think in innovative ways and help you create positive change. Mind Openers know how to ask good questions, and this makes you more receptive to ideas. When you are around a Mind Opener, you are unguarded and express opinions aloud, especially controversial ones that you might not be comfortable sharing with other friends. These friends broaden your perspective on life and make you a better person. If you need to challenge the conventional wisdom or shake up the status quo, spend a few hours talking with a Mind Opener.

MIND OPENERS IN ACTION:

- *"Jay is a long-time friend. He worked as a consultant with the U.S. government in Kazakhstan. I wanted to go visit him, and he suggested that I not only visit but sign up. So I did! I contacted the agency, and it turned out they were looking for volunteers with finance backgrounds. I took a leave of absence from my job and volunteered for three weeks. That's just like Jay. He said, 'Yeah, let's have fun, but why don't you think about it in a bigger context, and let's go do some good.' He was right; it was a once-in-a-lifetime experience and gave me a much greater insight into the country than if I would have just visited."*

  — Graham A., vice president of investments

- *"I have had a lot of back problems in my life and have never really taken proper steps to exercise and strengthen my back. My good friend Kathy kept hounding me to take Pilates with her. I didn't think I would like it, so I resisted. I finally gave in when she signed us up for a private class. Since that time, I have been going twice a week and have never felt better. I wouldn't have taken this step if it weren't for Kathy."*

  — Julie R., nurse practitioner

- *"Richard, one of my colleagues, really helps me make sure my decisions are sound because he asks good questions. I share one of my ideas or plans with him, and he pushes back and asks, 'Why should I believe this? Show me why.' Though sometimes it might feel like a pain, he challenges me to think about things differently or find a better way to do it. I really respect him for that."*

  — Lorraine K., systems administrator

WHO ARE YOUR MIND OPENERS?

_____

_____

_____

STRENGTHENING YOUR MIND OPENERS:

- Are you at an impasse with someone? Talk to your Mind Opener friends. They can help you see another perspective and view the situation from different vantage points.

- Give yourself time to think about your conversations with your Mind Openers. Try not to react or counter what they tell you right away. Instead, let it soak in a bit, and honor their perspectives, even though they may not be yours.

- When you formulate an idea or plan, before you implement it, ask your Mind Opener to play devil's advocate. Your plan might get better.

- Exchange ideas with your Mind Opener friends. They will welcome new ideas that make them think more. When you read an interesting book or see a compelling movie, recommend it to your Mind Opener friends. It will create stimulating conversation and probably expand your view.

CREATING NEW MIND OPENERS IN YOUR LIFE:

- At work, share ideas through brainstorming sessions or debriefings after a project is complete. Mind Openers will surface, ideas will become crisper, and your team will be more effective.

- Seek out people who have different opinions or beliefs than yours. Ask them questions. Take time to get to know them while seeking to understand their perspective.

- Put yourself in a new environment. While in this environment, reach out to others and let them know you are new and want to learn more. Some ideas are: Attend an event with a cultural theme that is different than your own, go hear alternative music, or take a continuing education class outside of your field of study or expertise.

- Say yes when a friend asks you to do something that is outside your comfort zone. At worst, you will have an interesting story to tell. At best, you will have learned more about yourself and your friend.

IF YOU ARE A MIND OPENER:

- Listen for extremes in the language of friends and acquaintances. This may signal opportunities for challenging conventional wisdom.

- Help your friends ask questions. When they pose good questions, help them reflect and focus on the answers.

- Experience is a great teacher. Seek opportunities to open minds through experience rather than attempting to convince others with words.

- Listen to your friends' thoughts and ideas. Share your ideas with them. These conversations will be stimulating for everyone. Skip the small talk, and dig into big topics. Your friends count on you to move beyond the surface and think big.

- Invite your friends to events or educational opportunities that they might not pursue on their own, and then have a follow-up discussion. This exchange will promote good conversation, and you will learn more about each other.

NAVIGATOR

Navigators are the friends who give you advice and keep you headed in the right direction. You go to them when you need guidance, and they talk through the pros and cons with you until you find an answer. In a difficult situation, you need a Navigator by your side. They help you see a positive future while keeping things grounded in reality. Any time you're at a crossroads and need help making a decision, you can look to a Navigator. They help you know who you are — and who you are not. They are the ideal friends to share your goals and dreams with; when you do, you will continue to learn and grow. When you ask Navigators for direction, they help you reach your destination.

NAVIGATORS IN ACTION:

- *"Andy has been my mentor for decades. After I lost my last job, we went out to dinner, and the entire discussion revolved around my future. I go to Andy when there is a lot of ambiguity in my life, and he helps me find clarity."*

  — Bill R., corporate buyer

- *"I never make a big decision without talking to my wife. She instinctively knows what's best for me. I think that's why I married her."*

  — Tyrone D., insurance agent

- *"I have a friend who is great when I am at a crossroads. I had been with an organization for seven years and was wavering about where I should go next. I just finished a master's program and was concerned about some of the pros and cons about a specific job I was considering. My friend was able to lay out why I should go for it and that it was a good and healthy risk. I valued her ability to support me in my decision and for all the right reasons. I ended up taking the job and couldn't be happier."*

  — Bonnie R., hospital administrator

- *"It seems that I can see the big picture but don't always know how to get there. Once I was complaining to my friend Joel that I felt stagnant at work and didn't know how to get to where I wanted to be. He asked me my goals, pulled out a pen, and started writing on a cocktail napkin. I still have that napkin on my desk as I work toward these goals each day."*

  — Ayanna B., training coordinator

WHO ARE YOUR NAVIGATORS?

_____

_____

_____

STRENGTHENING YOUR NAVIGATORS:

- If you are going through a period when you need to make big decisions, discuss your options with your Navigator friends. They will help you see all the possibilities as well as potential pitfalls.

- Ask Navigators about their own bumps in the road and the corresponding lessons they learned. They may like sharing not only advice, but the circumstances they faced in gaining their perspective on life.

- Share your dreams with your Navigator friends. By verbalizing your hopes and dreams, you increase the likelihood that they will come to fruition. Your Navigator friends will enjoy hearing them and may have some good ideas for taking the first step.

- If you are in a sticky situation, turn to your Navigator friends. They will help you get through it with grace and dignity.

CREATING NEW NAVIGATORS IN YOUR LIFE:

- You may very likely have a family member who is a Navigator. Ask your grandparents, parents, aunts, and uncles about their most memorable life-changing events. Ask them more about how they grew up. Discuss a decision you are facing with them.

- Ask people you admire to be your mentors. Find out how they got to where they are. Ask good questions. They are likely to feel honored and will make a point to think about your career or life path on a regular basis.

- Find out what your friends' life experiences and interests are. This will help you determine those who may guide you at different points in your life.

- Seek counsel from people you respect, such as clergy members, doctors, or former teachers. They will have your best interests at heart as they help you navigate through the situation at hand.

IF YOU ARE A NAVIGATOR:

- When temporary setbacks or small obstacles obscure your friends' view, help them focus on the big picture. Putting current events in perspective for them can ease their pain and get them focused on improving the immediate situation. Share a similar experience from your own life if possible.

- Your friends may turn to you as a sounding board. Make the time to listen and provide guidance. Be aware of opportunities that might help them achieve their goals, and share those opportunities with them.

- If your friends are facing a dilemma trying to choose the right path, help them think about the possible outcomes more clearly and uncover the best decision.

- Help your friends see the pros and cons of big decisions. They have probably turned to you in the past and trust you.

- When your friends have made important decisions or had successes, look for ways to celebrate their accomplishments. They will value this recognition.

- Share your dreams and visions with your friends. It will inspire them to think about their own dreams.

PART FOUR: BUILDING VITAL FRIENDSHIPS AT WORK

CHAPTER 12:
FAMILY TIES

When I speak with people who love their jobs and have vital friendships at work, they always talk about how their workgroup is like a family. Team members care about one another, listen, share secrets, talk about the latest news, have heated arguments, are sometimes jealous of each other, and even cry together. At times, these groups look more like a troubled family, but that's better than no family at all.

Chris, an energetic 18-year-old department supervisor for a major retail chain in Houston, makes it all seem so easy. He focuses most of his time and attention on building a family environment at work. Each morning, Chris makes a point to ask people how they're doing instead of barking orders. He spends time with his employees. He says, "We move the business *together.*" Chris knows this approach is working — not only because his team is producing more profit, but because of the enthusiasm in the air. Having no clue how many of his predecessors let decades pass without putting this kind of thought into managing their staff, Chris nonchalantly says, "The people you are around make you passionate about your job."

As Chris knows, if employees are distant from their peers, they don't get much done, and they are likely to leave their jobs. According to our studies, being ignored is one of the most psychologically damaging states for a human being. It's even worse than being treated poorly at work. If your manager essentially ignores you, the odds of your being engaged at work are an abysmal 1 in 50.

Of all the items we asked people to respond to, this one had the strongest linkage to job satisfaction: "My workgroup feels like a family." People who are fortunate enough to work in a family-like group report having stronger friendships across the board. They are far more likely to be in the thick of what's going on at work and can clearly see how their customers benefit from their close relationships.

DISTANT RELATIVES?

Fewer than 1 in 4 employees say their workgroup feels "like a family."

Jean, who manages a large call center, describes how easy it is for her to build a family-like atmosphere. Most of her employees are "like old friends." She makes it a point to stimulate dialogue among the group members every day, whether it's about work or an unrelated topic. Jean and her husband invite the entire team over to their house for dinner and drinks several times a year, and she has noticed that employees are now doing the same thing on their own. As a result, Jean describes how her group always looks for reasons to mingle and celebrate, and she reports that this strategy has resulted in record retention and performance numbers.

According to our research, we are tapping into only a small fraction of the potential for growth that lies in the development of friendships. Out of every 10 people that Gallup surveys, just two spend time with coworkers outside the workplace, and only 1 in 10 have built on workplace friendships to drive performance. The few people who consciously think about building workplace friendships are *2.5 times* more satisfied with their jobs.

CHAPTER 13:
THE WATER COOLER EFFECT

According to our research, workplaces with areas where employees can congregate, like dining and break areas, have twice as
many people with best friends at work. If you are involved in
shaping the layout of a new workspace or rearranging an exist-
ing area, consider this an opportunity to capitalize on the "water
cooler effect" by creating more conversations in your workplace.

In addition to the findings about dining and break areas,
our research revealed that workplaces with a physical layout
that makes it easy for people to socialize have significantly more
friendships. In fact, the effects of these environmental factors
were much stronger than we had originally guessed. You are
three times more likely to have a close-knit workgroup in this

kind of physical workplace environment. Unfortunately, only one-third of the people we asked feel that the physical layout of their workplace makes it easy for them to socialize.

BREAK ROOMS

Having areas to congregate can double the chances of having a best friend at work.

THE TERMINAL

In the late 1990s, retail giant Best Buy could hardly keep up with its own growth. Headquartered in the Minneapolis area, Best Buy's corporate staff was spread across 14 different locations, which posed a major challenge for this people-centric organization. The company's leadership figured it was time to build a new corporate campus and consolidate all 14 offices into one central location. They knew it would take a very innovative design to foster conversations and teamwork in a 1.6-million-square-foot building that needed to house 7,500 employees.

Best Buy decided to model the layout of an airport, with interconnected terminals. They labeled the buildings "Terminal A," "Terminal B," and so on, and then built the ultimate hub, or "Main Terminal." The Main Terminal would have three zones, dubbed "The Park," "The Café," and "The Neighborhood."

When you walk into Best Buy's Main Terminal, the first thing that strikes you is the bustling entryway. The only route for visitor or employee entry from the massive parking garage is through the middle of the Main Terminal. Even employees who work at the far end of Terminal D have to enter through this common area — although it is less than convenient. When you walk through the busy security area, you find yourself in the middle of one enormous room. This Main Terminal has soaring 30-foot ceilings, is surrounded by floor-to-ceiling glass, and spans the equivalent of almost four city blocks.

On any given morning, almost all the patio tables with umbrellas are occupied, with people talking, reading the newspaper, or working wirelessly from their laptops. Just beyond the tables is a full-sized Caribou Coffee with people waiting in line and chatting. Although indoors — and in suburban Minneapolis — the place has the feel of a sidewalk café in San Francisco. One reason this coffee shop is always packed is that it is the only place in the entire complex where employees can get coffee. Instead of placing coffee pots on each floor and in every building, Best Buy intentionally forces people to visit the terminal for their daily caffeine fix.

If you walk around the other side of this main area, you'll see foosball tables, pool tables, and several video game consoles near the large glass windows. Just beyond that is an outdoor sand volleyball court. None of this is unique — the place has the look and feel of a high-tech company, particularly in the Bay Area during the dotcom boom. Unfortunately, in many dotcom companies, employee play areas were just for show; you'd rarely see a foosball table in use, even though they were on the front of many companies' recruiting brochures. But at Best Buy, people actually play foosball or pool, and usually, every video game console is in use. And on the outer edges of the Main Terminal, there's a gift shop, bank, pharmacy, fitness center, health clinic, dry cleaner, and a bustling day care center.

The Main Terminal also houses a smaller building within a building. This is Best Buy's facility for meetings and management retreats. Instead of going off-site to a hotel or conference center, employees use this space for longer meetings. It's filled with large couches around a fireplace, a small creek with water flowing over rocks, and several small to mid-sized meeting rooms — some with whiteboard walls for brainstorming sessions. No one has a permanent office in this space; it's reserved for collaboration.

While it is impossible to quantify the precise impact of Best Buy's massive connecting hub, it's clear that it's stimulating thousands of additional interactions and conversations every day. As one Best Buy employee explained, "There always seems to be an energy in the building." You could call it a water cooler for the 21st century.

KNOCKING DOWN WALLS

You are three times as likely to have a close-knit workgroup if the physical environment makes it easy to socialize.

Unfortunately, only one-third of the people we studied report working in such an environment.

Best Buy is not alone. Over the past decade, many organizations have designed their buildings to encourage conversations and interaction. One of the world's largest software companies has modeled its headquarters after a large ship. The building is shaped like a long narrow boat encased in glass. Every employee, including the top executives, sits in a cubicle with natural sunlight streaming in from both sides.

According to our research, nearly one-third of employees cannot see the outside from their workspace — and people in this group are 86% more likely to be disengaged in their jobs. The good news is, employers are finally starting to realize the importance of architecture, and they are taking this into account before construction starts. The bad news is, many people work in older buildings that were designed during the days when workspaces had more walls, and people were rewarded with plush, remote corner offices that created additional distance from the masses.

If you work in a building with imperfect architecture, it will take a bit more effort and creativity to foster vital friendships. Many organizations depend on "virtual" water coolers. That is, they encourage people to bring the conversation with them wherever they go, helping others connect. Regular events where people can catch up and meet others can also serve as venues for ad-hoc conversations. Organizations filled with "best friends" are always trying new things: weekly or monthly social hours, dinners hosted by managers in their homes with their workgroups, outings to events in the area, involvement in community service groups, or larger parties for special holidays and events. These workplaces have one thing in common: They try anything to start a conversation.

CHAPTER 14:
PLUGGING IN

Imagine this: Someone you recently met invites you to dinner at his home, and you accept. The following Wednesday evening, you arrive at the agreed-upon time. As you were expecting, your host opens the door and lets you in. He then points you in the direction of the dining room and walks off in the opposite direction, telling you he will return. Slightly taken aback by this lack of hospitality, you wander around and eventually find the dining room.

After waiting for about 15 minutes, you get tired of standing and decide to sit down at the table. A woman and two small children are watching television in a nearby room. They can clearly see you waiting, but they don't acknowledge your presence.

One of the children stares at you for a few moments, providing a glimmer of hope, but then walks right by you on her way to the kitchen and doesn't say a word.

Thirty minutes after your arrival, the guy who invited you to dinner has yet to return. Even though you normally would have walked out by this point, the entire scene is so bizarre that you stay around out of curiosity, wanting to know what's wrong with this family.

Then, when you thought you had seen it all, your host finally enters the room carrying a stack of books and manuals. He sets them on the table and pleasantly says, "Let me know if you have any questions" and leaves the room. You start to peruse the manual on top and see the title: *How to Use Your Gas Range*. The next manual is titled: *KRC 542: Microwave Oven*. The rest of the stack contains a few standard cookbooks.

This scene, albeit fictional, is comparable to what happens to many new employees when they enter their new workplace; they are essentially given directions on how to cook their own meal and then left alone. Just ask Stephen, a project manager who thought he had finally found the ideal job. Even though his new position required moving to a city more than 500 miles from his hometown, Stephen jumped at the opportunity after talking to the recruiter and reading the job description. He was sure he would love the job, and he was full of excitement when he arrived.

On his first day, someone from Human Resources showed Stephen to his office, left him with a couple of product manuals, and told him to read them. During his first week, that was all he did — peruse company manuals. Each day, as the noon hour neared, Stephen quietly hoped someone would ask him to join them for lunch in the company's cafeteria so he would not have to eat alone. No such luck. No one even stopped by to chat or help him get acquainted with his new job and new city. The following Monday, he called in "sick." He did the same the next day. Then, on Wednesday, Stephen submitted his resignation after 10 days on the job.

This story illustrates why it's critical for people who are new to a group to get plugged into a network of potential friends right away. Once these personal connections are made, they usually last. The best online and distance degree programs require new students to spend a few intensive weeks together before they begin communicating virtually. Once you have gotten to know someone face-to-face, working with them at a distance can be very effective. Without these personal connections, you would be working with relative strangers.

One professional services company I work with brings a group of 15 to 30 new associates together in one location every few months and provides them with two to three weeks of learning and socializing. They take the group to dinners, sporting events, and other area attractions. This builds bonds with co-workers that last for decades — even when they go back to work in different cities. They are wired into a network from day one. According to our research, organizations that help new employees make friends could double the chances of those new employees being satisfied at work.

UNPLUGGED?

Just 1 in 4 employees had someone help them make new friends when they started their last job.

Other organizations have less formal programs that pair new employees with mentors or advisors who think about the new employee's personal and professional growth. A division of consumer products giant Procter & Gamble requires new team members to spend a full hour talking with each person on the team they are joining. The employees are specifically directed to talk about their friends, families, hobbies, and other outside interests — *any work-related topics are off limits* for this initial hour. As a result, members of the team build trust and relationships much faster than they had in previous jobs. And when questions or issues arise later, it is much easier for new members of the group to ask those questions. In the words of one team member, "This made it much easier for me, as a new person, to get involved and seek advice."

PLUGGING IN BEFORE MEETINGS

Regardless of whether you love or dread meetings, they do provide a venue for getting to know your colleagues. However, when a meeting starts, most of us have a tendency to jump right into things. I am as impatient as anyone, and I cannot stand meetings that run unnecessarily long. But whenever you have new people in the group — or have not met for some time — it pays to open things up on a different note.

A previous manager of mine, Don, started every meeting with a brief activity. He thought people should get to know each other before diving into an agenda. The first thing Don would do is distribute a few pieces of paper to each person in the room. Every sheet had the following headings printed across the top: Name, Hobbies, Personal Success, and Professional Success. Don would then open the meeting by asking everyone to answer these four questions:

- *What name do you prefer to be called?*

- *What are one or two of your favorite activities or hobbies outside of work?*

- *What is one recent personal success you have had?*

- *What is one recent professional success you have had?*

At first, this seemed a bit odd to me, and perhaps a waste of time, but it certainly helped us become acquainted and settle in before we tackled pressing work topics. It even gave me a refresher course on people's names. After attending a few of these meetings, I began to notice other colleagues who shared my interests, which led to follow-up conversations after the meeting. A couple of my strongest workplace friendships started off this way, and it's unlikely we would have connected in the first place if Don hadn't kicked off every meeting with a few good questions.

This is one of the most common ways a vital friendship is formed at work — discovering a coworker with common interests or beliefs. The best workgroups we have studied engage in passionate conversations and e-mail discussions about non-work topics. This helps the group bond and makes it stronger.

PARTING THOUGHTS

In his final hours, Franklin Delano Roosevelt was thinking about the next great frontier, one he felt was critical to civilization's survival: cultivating the science of human relationships. Based on the research that we conducted for this book and that of leading academics, the insights of people we interviewed, and my own personal experiences, it looks like President Roosevelt was right. Vast, untapped potential exists if we are able to improve the quality of our friendships.

Throughout my life, I have taken my closest relationships for granted. A few years ago, if you were to ask me if I *needed* stronger friendships, my answer would have been a resounding no. I already had several strong personal friendships and a couple good friends at work. Furthermore, I didn't see why my work and personal circles of friends should cross over — it seemed cleaner to keep them separated.

My assumptions were wrong. In hindsight, I had several mal-nourished friendships. They were by no means starved, but I had spent very little time consciously improving my best friendships. And I hadn't spent much time trying to develop new ones. Apparently, this is the norm. A 2001 study found that even the *very loneliest* people didn't realize they needed more social support.

After thinking about my own situation more consciously, I discovered several vital friendships sneaking beneath my radar: friends from college who always opened my mind to new ideas or political views; a few people I did not talk to frequently, but who were always there to give me great advice when it mattered; a couple of "fun" buddies who turned out to be great Energizers in my life; several Collaborators who were emerging friends; and even a few family bonds, the vitality of which I had seriously underestimated. Another eye opener was that I need to find a few Connectors to help me crawl out of my social cave every once in a while.

Once I began to understand the critical roles friends play in my life, it changed my perspective quickly. As I started to describe to my friends what they bring to my life, I found that doing so lifted their spirits even more than my own. Later, I experienced a similar sense of pride as others explained the Vital Roles I play in their lives. Each one of these conversations was a critical moment in our relationship, as it honed in on the strong points of our friendship and gave us crystal-clear expectations of each other.

As you begin to look at your own friendships through a new lens, I hope you have a similar experience. Based on the interviews we have conducted with groups of vital friends, here are a few changes that might occur as you strengthen your vital friendships:

- an improvement in your physical health

- more happiness on a day-to-day basis

- increased engagement and achievement in your job

- clear expectations between you and your spouse, relatives, friends, and coworkers

Building on your vital friendships can improve countless facets of your life if, and only if, you dedicate your attention to the positive roles people *do* play in your life instead of focusing on what they *don't* bring to your life. This one key will help you unlock the potential within each friendship.

Start there. Then focus your attention on *what you contribute*. Even though the Vital Friends Assessment focuses on what different friends bring to your life, it is critical that you figure out what you add to each friend's life. Whether you want to build more friendships, create stronger friendships, or both, this is an essential step. Every friendship requires give and take, and what you *give* is likely to be even more powerful than what you get.

APPENDIXES
AND REFERENCES

APPENDIX A:
YOUR QUESTIONS

If you have taken the Vital Friends Assessment and started to explore the roles different friends play in your life, chances are you have a few questions. In the following pages, you will find answers to 12 of the most common inquiries I have received. Whether you're curious about how to use the results of the assessment or simply wondering how to initiate a conversation on this topic, I hope you find this brief Q&A useful.

Next, the case study in Appendix B offers an expanded response to the most common questions I hear from organizational leaders. They are typically eager to know why relationships, particularly between leaders and their constituencies, are so bad today. And they want to know what can be done, at an organizational level, to remedy this epidemic.

Q: **If none of my friends plays a particular role, should I go out and find a friend who does?**

A: Each Vital Role is linked to an increase in life satisfaction and workplace engagement, so it would likely benefit you to have at least one friend who plays each role. For example, some people have reported that many of their friends play the role of Energizer while none of their friends play another role — perhaps Navigator. If you have similar results, this is an opportunity to look within yourself and reflect on why you seek out one type of role in a friend, or more importantly, whether or not you are allowing your friends to play a role that is not showing up. In this example, if Navigator is not present in any of your friendships, ask yourself how well you accept guidance or advice from your friends.

Q: **Should I keep my assessment results confidential?**

A: No! The purpose of this instrument is to create discussion about the positive aspects of your relationships with the people you care about most. Therefore, we encourage you to share as much as you feel comfortable sharing. The assessment is only valuable if it leads to dialogue with friends, coworkers, and loved ones.

Q: How can my friends access the Vital Friends website?

A: Each book contains one unique access code that allows you to register and create your own personalized website on www.vitalfriends.com. The website is built around you and your network of friends. Therefore, your friends will need their own copy of the book to build their virtual network and take the assessment.

Gallup has conducted assessments for decades, and we have found that if an assessment like this is taken with no educational context, it has little benefit. There are thousands of inexpensive "tests" available, especially with the growth of the Internet. A few are solid assessments, but unless they are coupled with some educational context, even the best ones turn into glorified horoscopes.

This is one of the many reasons why Gallup includes this assessment within the context of a book or professional development program. We want to ensure that your friends understand the concept and power of vital friendships versus simply taking a quick web test (e.g., the ones you receive via e-mail or see in a magazine).

The Vital Friends Assessment is the product of a multimillion dollar research and development project that draws on decades of Gallup research. Giving this book to friends, or even recommending that they check it out, sends a message. It tells your friends that they matter in your life and gives them the opportunity to explore their own friendships.

Q: What if I am too busy? How can I invest in friendships?

A: You have the most room for development within your strongest friendships today. Think of your best friendships both in the workplace and in your personal life. Initially, dedicate your attention on opportunities that will enhance these relationships.

If you are trying to develop new friendships, begin in the workplace or the place where you spend most of your time. Invite potential friends to activities that you are already involved in. Maximize your time by including people you would like to get to know better in lunch plans or golf outings. New friendships cannot develop without the investment of time, but you can make the most of your time by integrating an activity that you are already doing with an opportunity to create or further develop a friendship.

Q: **Are there friends I am better off not having at all — ones who are not "vital"? How can I tell the difference?**

A: If any of your relationships are based on negativity or focused on what each person is *not* bringing to the relationship, try making a shift to the positive through discussion and conscious action. If you try this for an extended period of time and have no luck, it might be time to give up. Someone who constantly brings negativity into your life is not a vital friend.

Q: **Does proximity matter in vital friendships? Do friends need to live nearby?**

A: Initially, our research team thought proximity could be a major issue. And with increased emphasis on "virtual teams" and telecommuting, we wondered if this was leading to fewer friendships on the job.

In our first rounds of testing the Vital Friends Assessment, we included several items to assess the impact of proximity on life satisfaction and workplace engagement. The correlations were weak — indicating that physical proximity was not a key influencer of any of these important outcomes. Other studies have found similar results. One study found that proximity does not cause liking; it simply amplifies the effect of other variables and events.

This certainly does not minimize the role of proximity in more casual relationships. Proximity matters, but maybe not in the case of vital friendships. *Proximity matters at the time of forming friendships but not necessarily in maintaining them.* Strong ties remain strong regardless of distance. Lack of proximity might lead to slower friendship formation, but given sufficient time to develop and sufficient opportunities to interact on a one-on-one basis, it might not be a deciding variable at all.

Q: Two of my friends play the same Vital Role in my life. How do I compare them?

A: Each friend is unique and brings different things to your life. Two friends who play the same role might contribute in very different ways in terms of the specific things they do for you. The important thing is to value friends for the unique qualities they have and the roles they play in your life. The Vital Friends Assessment was designed to increase the quality of an interpersonal relationship through dialogue, not to compare the roles of two different friends.

Q: **Does having a close friend at work really make me feel better about my pay?**

A: In 2003, we studied people who were in similar income bands to understand the correlation between friendship and perceptions of pay. We found that employees who had close friends at work had a much more favorable perception of their pay, when compared to people without close friends at work. The significant improvement in perception was around 1.75 to 2 times higher than what it would be if the employee could not claim a close friendship at work. The improvement in pay perception increased for the lower income bands, reaching a 200% increase for the lowest income band. These numbers suggest that close friendships at work could provide a form of intangible compensation for employees.

Q: **Is there really a payoff in focusing on friendships that are already strong?**

A: Yes. During the course of our study, we discovered that people who "strongly agree" with the statement "I have a best friend at work" were significantly more satisfied with their lives than people who merely agreed or were neutral. The poll also indicated that 48% of people are either neutral or a little better than neutral in terms of overall satisfaction with their relationships — they are in relationships that are good, but not necessarily vital.

Having the right expectations of your friends is everything. If your expectations don't align with what your friends are capable of, the relationship is doomed. If your expectations are in alignment with the things each person can bring to your life, the friendship is poised to thrive.

Try this and see what happens:

If you have a friend who doesn't really push you to do more — but you know that you can trust her with any secret — tell her your secrets and look to someone else to help you realize your dreams.

If you have one friend who always gives you good advice, go to him for direction. Don't go to another friend who listens empathetically to what you say but doesn't offer much guidance. Go to her when you need someone to accept you for who you are.

If you are out of work and need a job, talk to your friend who has a broad network of connections. Don't ask for help from your introverted friend who may lack that network.

Q: **How does Gallup's Vital Friends Assessment compare and contrast with the Clifton StrengthsFinder?**

A: The Clifton StrengthsFinder, a 180-item online assessment that measures a person's natural talents, is all about you and your *individual development*. The Vital Friends Assessment is about your *one-on-one relationships*. It uncovers the Vital Roles each friend plays in your life.

Q: **I have a lot of family responsibilities. How can I focus on my friendships when my family takes up so much time?**

A: Family members are likely to be some of your most vital friends. Include your spouse, children, parents, siblings, or other relatives in the assessment. Use this as an opportunity to strengthen these relationships and to tell those closest to you what they mean in your life. Often, we put on our best face for strangers and friends outside the home. Because we feel safe in our home environment, we might not work as hard at developing these friendships. Use the Vital Friends Assessment to reflect on all relationships and to spend time on those closest to you.

Q: **I feel like a conversation on this topic could be awkward. Any suggestions?**

A: According to our research, when you tell another person how much you value his or her friendship, it improves the relationship dramatically. Those who have told a friend how much they value a friendship in the past month are 48% more likely to be "extremely satisfied with the friendships" in their lives. So even if it is difficult at first, initiating these conversations is essential if you want to build stronger relationships.

To make things easier, start with a loved one. For example, tell your spouse exactly why she is so important in your life. If your marriage makes you a better person, leader, and dad, let her know. Take her out to dinner, and focus all of your energy on describing the Vital Roles she plays in your life. If she's an Energizer, explain how you had a lively interaction with her last week and were in a better mood as a result. If she's a Mind Opener, tell her about a long-held view of yours that she has influenced or changed. Do not spare any detail. And help her understand how she can play that role *even more* in your life.

At a minimum, having this conversation will lift the other person's spirits. If you pour your heart into this, it might end up being one of the most powerful and memorable moments in your relationship. Then do the same thing with another very close friend. Your comfort level will increase as you have more of these discussions with friends and colleagues.

If you have difficultly "speaking your heart" with certain people, try another variation: speak your mind. Instead of jumping into what this person contributes to your life emotionally, open up with the facts. Focus on the things he does to boost your achievement. If he plays the role of a Builder in your life and keeps you moving every day, let him know. Describe a situation when he motivated you to achieve more. And make sure to let him know how he can do more of this in the next few months, years, and beyond.

Whether these conversations with vital friends happen at home, at work, in a restaurant, or at a ballgame, make sure these are not unique events or one-time conversations. Research has shown that continuous follow-through is essential to bring about real growth. See if you can have at least one conversation when you speak your heart or your mind every month.

Go ahead and schedule these interactions like you would a doctor's appointment — it might be equally important for your health. Set reminders to follow through with more conversations. Once you've done this with most of your vital friends, go through your list again, always zeroing in on the additional things each person is contributing to your life. Trust me, no one is going to get sick of hearing it as long as your words are specific and sincere. Before long, your friends and family members will be coming to you to talk about the roles *you play* in their lives.

A CASE STUDY: CAN LEADERS SET THE TONE?

Building stronger workplace friendships is a formidable challenge for any organization. On average, *just 17%* of employees feel that their organization's leadership encourages friendships.

To study the roots of this problem, I decided to take a closer look at the automobile industry, in part because of its history of having poor employee relations, particularly with blue-collar workers. Dating back to the industry's origins, Henry Ford himself went as far as to hire heavy-handed spies to keep frontline employees in check. Ford was also known to have his own private army, with machine guns and tear gas, to intimidate employees and prevent them from unionizing. This led to an environment in which it was almost impossible to have positive relationships on the job.

When I spoke with former Chrysler President Thomas Stallkamp, he explained how this adversarial culture evolved. Stallkamp described the way many of these issues stemmed from "the old command and control theory" and "enormous problems with unions." He detailed how hostile relationships broke the tire companies, steel industry, and many other large manufacturing industries during the 20th century. In each of these cases, management and unions "felt they had to deal with each other in a very adversarial, confrontational method." According to Stallkamp, this in turn affected employee relations and the way customers were treated.

Every person I spoke with from one of the traditional Big Three automakers (Ford, General Motors, and Chrysler) described a distinct "us versus them" mentality. The unwritten rules said that managers should be friends only with managers, hourly employees only with hourly employees. And there should be very little in between. According to Mike, who worked on a Ford assembly line for more than 40 years, this "class system" bore a striking resemblance to the military. Mike described how the tension between management and union workers led to the production of automobiles that "weren't of the quality that people really wanted." Instead of taking pride in producing top-quality cars and trucks, many of the people assembling vehicles were completely disengaged in their jobs, and some were actively trying to sabotage the employer they hated so much.

Solange De Santis, a veteran business reporter I interviewed, went undercover and worked on a General Motors production line for 18 months. In her book *Life on the Line*, she described a "semimilitaristic division of white collar from blue collar in the plant." De Santis was constantly reminded of her lowly status. She explained how the "white shirts" (management and front-line workers literally wore different colors of uniforms) worked in nice, cool, air-conditioned cubicles, while hourly workers were stuck in a "sweatbox." In addition to being treated like animals, hourly workers were forced to park in a separate lot far behind the building and could not have their paychecks direct-deposited like salaried employees.

Even after enduring these conditions for months, De Santis was careful not to blame management, the company, or the unions exclusively. When management did offer a small concession, such as providing free coffee, De Santis' fellow hourly co-workers would take two to three times as much coffee as they could possibly drink, simply to get back at the company.

It's important to note that this was not a world completely devoid of friendships. During my interviews with the autoworkers, I learned of several close relationships, particularly among the hourly rank-and-file. Unfortunately, when I asked workers what they talked about, I learned that they might be more like "belly-ache buddies" than friends. Their conversations were almost entirely based on complaining about their employer — these were clearly not productive friendships.

In the end, the division between union workers and managers was so fierce that it led to severe violence and eventually contributed to one of the greatest economic failures on record. (It has also been the subject of numerous books and movies.) This division also created a deadly cold war, not with other automakers, but between workers and management. Following a 2005 incident in which a disgruntled employee walked into his workplace at a Jeep assembly plant, killed a supervisor, shot himself, and wounded others, a 30-year veteran of the plant commented that virtually everyone thinks plant management is out to get them.

A DIFFERENT APPROACH

In sharp contrast to the conditions that prevailed in Ford, General Motors, and Chrysler plants, Japanese automaker Toyota adopted a different approach in the latter half of the 20th century. From its early years, one of the core "Toyota Precepts" was teamwork, and Toyota encouraged an open environment with regular collaboration between the front lines and Toyota's leadership. In Big Three factories, workers on the line were expected to obey orders and to keep questions to a minimum. In Japan, Toyota's line workers were encouraged to be creative and challenge the status quo.

Could this approach help Toyota compete with the Big Three? It certainly was an uphill battle. According to one industry insider, General Motors' global lead over Toyota in the 1980s was "comparable to a football team having a 99-0 lead at halftime." This didn't stop Toyota from trying. The Japanese automaker was able to extend its core philosophy as it went into direct competition with the Big Three, eventually building manufacturing plants in the United States. When Toyota opened its first wholly owned and operated plant in Georgetown, Kentucky, the man who later became the company's CEO walked the lengthy assembly line every day and spent hours getting to know his employees. This was symbolic of the approach that made Toyota's culture great — and the organization was about to reap huge dividends as a result.

The employee empowerment approach at Toyota was the antithesis of the average General Motors plant. Instead of having special shirts for management, as in GM plants, even the top person in a Toyota plant wore the same uniform as the frontline workers. Toyota plants had four levels of leadership within each plant, as opposed to 15 levels of hierarchy in Big Three factories. In the Toyota system, each employee had a group leader with a very clear assignment: to get work done *through* or *with* each employee. They were not foremen, but instead were there to help others learn and grow. Executives, managers, and employees were constantly nurturing the relationships within the organization.

According to Toyota executive Mike Morrison, the company expects every frontline employee to "shape and create their own work." Employees are empowered to do what it takes to innovate and increase speed — and this autonomy creates ownership and pride throughout the organization. Early evidence suggests Toyota's approach is working.

Almost 20 years after it started manufacturing cars on U.S. soil, Toyota has yet to see a plant unionize, a near-impossible feat, given the power of the autoworkers unions and Toyota's unprecedented growth. Unions are usually created because of relationships gone bad, which explains why they might continue to serve a purpose at General Motors — yet are unnecessary at Toyota. The difference between a union and non-union environment also has direct connections to each car buyer's pocketbook. In her book *The End of Detroit*, Micheline Maynard estimates that United Autoworkers Union (UAW) contracts cost the Big Three a $1,200 penalty for every car sold, while Toyota has no such issues.

It is important to note that Toyota's focus on building reliable, quality cars has also been unparalleled. They have figured out how to build more cars at a lower cost in less time than U.S.-based automakers. Undoubtedly, the widely publicized process, quality, and engineering improvements have been a key catalyst behind Toyota's success. Yet people are quick to underestimate how Toyota's open and collaborative environment contributed to this increase in quality and subsequent come-from-behind victory. As of 2005, the market capitalization, or overall value, of Toyota *was more than five times the enterprise value* of General Motors or Ford.

UNTAPPED POTENTIAL

Toyota's leadership was able to create an environment in which friendships were possible, but like most other companies, they did not directly encourage closer relationships between employees. Fostering relationships on the job may not seem like something that should be part of a company's or leader's mission, but perhaps it should be.

Several companies Gallup works with have been able to dramatically increase the number and strength of friendships within their organization. When they do, more engaged employees and customers, as well as profits, usually follow. Our evidence also suggests that an increase in best friends at work could lead to more creativity and innovation throughout the organization.

APPENDIX C:
DEVELOPMENT OF THE VITAL FRIENDS ASSESSMENT: A TECHNICAL REPORT

Prepared by

James K. Harter, Ph.D.

Timothy D. Hodges, MS

Jason A. Carr, Ph.D.

THE GALLUP ORGANIZATION
1001 Gallup Drive
Omaha, NE 68102

February 2006

INTRODUCTION

The world is full of dyads — numerous individual, one-on-one relationships that shape our interactions and feelings each day. Yet not enough research has been done to understand how to categorize or summarize the meaning of the regular interactions in our lives. Many of the most important dyads in our lives are our friendships. They take on many dimensions. In the series of studies described in this report, we attempted to apply measurement to the dimensionality of friendships.

The Gallup Organization has accumulated studies on the role of friendships in the workplace — and the world — for decades. These studies have included both qualitative and quantitative methods. Qualitative methods include thousands of interviews and focus groups with productive individuals and teams. These interviews enable researchers to listen to successful individuals describe why they are successful. Such methods have been particularly useful in developing theories and designing questions.

Quantitative methods include asking questions and accumulating and analyzing numerical data to draw inferences from responses to questions. Decades of such research were available as a starting point in developing theories and writing items that would potentially tap into the dimensionality of friendships. Gallup meta-analyses continue to reveal a meaningful relationship between friendships at work and numerous performance outcomes (Harter, Schmidt, & Killham, 2003), including customer loyalty/engagement, safety, and profitability. The goal of this project was to take the understanding of friendships to another level by studying the dimensionality of work and non-work friendships.

PHASE I

We conducted our research in several iterations, starting in 2004 and finishing in 2005. In early 2004, we began thinking about the dimensions of friendships by conducting qualitative interviews and writing statements that described the friendships we were studying. We wrote hundreds of descriptive statements about work and non-work friendships, knowing we would not be able to efficiently administer all of them to any one sample of respondents. Our team of item writers met several times, reviewed the statements, rewrote them, and deleted those that were either redundant or not understandable to a wide cross-section of people. Then in June 2004, we began our quantitative analysis with 144 statements that described the variety of friendships we had observed. The 144 items conceptually fit into 10 dimensions ranging from "guidance" to "fun" to "closeness." The names of the dimensions (or friendship "roles") have evolved over time, indicative of our item revisions and interactions with users of the assessment.

PHASE II

We began our quantitative analysis at call centers in Houston, Texas, and Irvine, California. We purposefully picked the most diverse call centers we could find, where employees ranged greatly in race, gender, and age. We asked 159 respondents to identify their closest friend at work, their closest friend away from work, and an acquaintance. Then we asked them to complete a 144-item web-based survey on each of the three people they had identified. Surveys were conducted from June 2-15, 2004. A 5-point agreement scale accompanied each statement, with 5="strongly agree"…1="strongly disagree," and a sixth "don't know/does not apply" option.

Example:	Strongly Disagree				Strongly Agree
_____ is very open to my ideas.	1	2	3	4	5

In addition to the 144 Vital Friends items, we began the survey by measuring each respondent's subjective well-being (SWB, on a 5-item scale: Diener, 1984) and his or her engagement at work (Q^{12} scale: Harter, Schmidt, & Killham, 2003). SWB items included: "In most ways, my life is close to ideal," "The conditions of my life are excellent," "I am satisfied with my life," "So far, I have gotten the important things I want in my life," and "If I could live my life over, I would change almost nothing." Engagement at work has been studied extensively and is substantially related to a variety of performance outcomes, including business unit profitability, productivity, employee retention, customer engagement, and safety. Gallup's Q^{12} includes items measuring the extent to which employees are involved in and enthusiastic about their work. The Q^{12} has been completed by more than eight million employees worldwide. Below is a listing of the Q^{12} items:

Gallup Q^{12} Items
On a scale of 1 to 5, where 5 is strongly agree, and 1 is strongly disagree, please indicate your level of agreement with each of the following items.

Q01.	I know what is expected of me at work.
Q02.	I have the materials and equipment I need to do my work right.
Q03.	At work, I have the opportunity to do what I do best every day.
Q04.	In the last seven days, I have received recognition or praise for doing good work.
Q05.	My supervisor, or someone at work, seems to care about me as a person.
Q06.	There is someone at work who encourages my development.
Q07.	At work, my opinions seem to count.
Q08.	The mission or purpose of my company makes me feel my job is important.
Q09.	My associates or fellow employees are committed to doing quality work.
Q10.	I have a best friend at work.
Q11.	In the last six months, someone at work has talked to me about my progress.
Q12.	This last year, I have had opportunities at work to learn and grow.

Once responses to the survey were completed for the work friend, non-work friend, and acquaintance, we tabulated the data and studied the relationship between each item and both SWB and engagement at work. We also studied differences between the work friend, the non-work friend, and the acquaintance. We deleted items that did not meet both of the following criteria:

- significant correlation to either workplace engagement or SWB
- significant difference between closest friend (both work friend and non-work friend) and acquaintance

PHASE III

When Phase II was finished, we had retained 101 items. To expand the types of employees studied, we administered the 101 items (plus SWB and workplace engagement) to 152 English-speaking professional services firm employees worldwide from October 18-November 8, 2004.

We again asked each respondent to identify his or her closest friend at work and his or her closest friend away from work, and to complete the assessment on each. Differences between closest friends and acquaintances were extremely large for the items retained following Phase II; therefore, we did not collect the acquaintance data in Phase III.

At the conclusion of Phase III, we retained items that significantly correlated with their hypothesized dimensions (role) and that significantly correlated with either workplace engagement or SWB.

PHASE IV

After Phase III ended, we had retained 66 items. To again expand the types of employees studied and the size of our instrument development sample, we administered the 66-item instrument to 1,588 randomly selected U.S. adults, 18 years of age or older, from Gallup's panel of 17,855 households. The sample was 55% female, 45% male; 83% Caucasian, 17% minority; and the average age was 44.21 years.

Once again, items were studied in relationship to the dimension (role) they were intended to measure and in relation to workplace engagement and SWB. Additionally, we conducted the above analyses for subgroups of race, gender, and age so that items could be tested as to criterion relevancy for a variety of demographic groups. We retained 65 of the 66 items. Table 1 presents the number of items per Vital Friends role and the average item correlation to its own role (its own role score minus the item being studied) for work and non-work friends. Table 1 also includes the Cronbach's Alpha reliabilities, which represent the coefficient of equivalence. Reliabilities of .70 or higher are generally considered high. Results of the analyses indicate the reliabilities for individual Vital Friends roles are quite high — generally well above .80, and exceeding .90 in some cases.

Table 1: Statistics For Each Vital Friends Role					
		Average Item to Theme*		Cronbach's Alpha Reliability	
Vital Friends Role	# of Items	Work Friend	Non-Work Friend	Work Friend	Non-Work Friend
Builder	9	.71	.71	.92	.92
Champion	7	.66	.58	.87	.81
Collaborator	10	.61	.58	.88	.85
Companion	10	.68	.63	.91	.88
Connector	5	.63	.57	.83	.79
Energizer	8	.65	.63	.88	.87
Mind Opener	7	.61	.60	.85	.84
Navigator	9	.68	.68	.90	.90
*Correlation corrected for part-whole overlap					

TEST-RETEST RELIABILITY

In the summer of 2005, a preliminary test-retest study was conducted in which 91 participants were asked to rate a friend using the web-based Vital Friends Assessment. The participants were asked to rate the same friend again about two weeks later. The period between test and retest administrations for each of the participants ranged from 15 to 42 days. Participants were able to view the role reports generated after each administration.

The results of the test-retest study were analyzed in several ways. First, the test-retest reliabilities of the individual Vital Friends roles were examined (see Table 2). The test-retest reliabilities were generally high; the reliabilities ranged from 0.78 to 0.85. The mean of the test-retest reliabilities was 0.82.

Next, for each of the participants, the ranking of the entire set of roles at test was correlated with the ranking of the entire set of roles at retest. The median Spearman's rho value was 0.62. The average Spearman's rho value was 0.54.

Table 2: Vital Friends Role Test-Retest Reliabilities	
Vital Friends Role	Test-Retest Reliability
Builder	0.83
Champion	0.81
Collaborator	0.84
Companion	0.83
Connector	0.78
Energizer	0.82
Mind Opener	0.79
Navigator	0.85

More details on test-retest reliability are provided in Carr (2006).

FACTOR ANALYSES

In addition to studying the intercorrelation among the items in the Vital Friends Assessment and correlating each item to its respective theme, factor analyses were used during each iteration of quantitative instrument development (Phases II through IV) as a guide to reduce the redundancy of items in each role and to maximize the independence of the measured constructs. Principal Components factor analysis with both Varimax and Direct Oblimin rotation was used. Results of both the Varimax and Direct Oblimin rotations were similar. Factor analysis conducted on the 65-item instrument indicated seven interpretable factors, all with eigenvalues greater than 1 (for work and non-work friends). The factor analysis revealed a large first factor. The items included in the first factor (which include items psychologically indicative of "mentoring" friendships) were factor analyzed separately, revealing two distinguishable constructs that we call "Builder" and "Navigator." Separately, these two friendship roles distinguish between those who provide a "motivational" role versus a "guiding" role. Two example items that distinguish between these two factors are: "____ pushes me to achieve more" and "I would not make an important decision without ____." Therefore, we retained an eight-factor solution (the seven-factor solution, with the first factor split into two roles), knowing there would be slightly more overlap between "Builder" and "Navigator" than among the remaining six roles.

CRITERION RELATEDNESS

Table 3 shows the correlation of each Vital Friends role to engagement at work and SWB for both the work friend and non-work friend who were being rated. Correlations in each case are positive and significant. Vital Friends roles correlated most positively to engagement at work (for the work friends who were rated), and to SWB (for the non-work friends who were rated). This is consistent with theory, in that we would expect the work friendships to correspond with levels of employee engagement.

And the non-work friendships rated more positively should be associated with higher levels of life satisfaction for the respondents. The correlation of Vital Friends role to engagement varies from .22 to .28. The correlation of Vital Friends role to SWB varies from .12 to .21. It is important to assess the practical meaning of these relationships.

Table 3: Correlation of Vital Friends Roles to Workplace Engagement and Subjective Well-Being				
Correlation* to:				
Vital Friends Role	Work Friend		Non-Work Friend	
	Engagement**	SWB***	Engagement**	SWB***
Builder	.27	.10	.14	.18
Champion	.22	.09	.13	.17
Collaborator	.28	.15	.13	.20
Companion	.25	.11	.08	.17
Connector	.24	.08	.14	.12
Energizer	.24	.09	.14	.21
Mind Opener	.28	.13	.16	.21
Navigator	.28	.12	.10	.19

* (n=1,588) correlations greater than .06 are significant (p<.05); correlations are corrected for dependent variable measurement error
** Workplace engagement measured by mean of Gallup Q^{12} (Buckingham & Coffman, 1999; Harter, Schmidt, & Killham, 2003)
*** Subjective Well-Being (SWB) measured by mean of five-item SWB scale (Diener, 1984)

Applying Gallup's proprietary formula to the Q^{12} items in this sample, 31% are "engaged" in their work, 54% are "not engaged," and 15% are "actively disengaged." Those who rated their closest work friend in the top quartile on the "Collaborator" role had much higher overall engagement at work: 54% "engaged," 39% "not engaged," and 7% "actively disengaged." People with "Collaborators" at work have a 74% greater chance of being engaged at work. This is the practical effect of a .28 correlation.

Similar relationships are seen in the additional roles. Each role contributes positively to engagement at work.

For non-work friends, the correlation of the "Energizer" role and SWB (life satisfaction) is .21. For the overall sample, 40% of respondents had SWB of 4.00 or higher (on a 5-point scale); 52% of those who rated their closest non-work friend in the top quartile on "Energizer" had high SWB (4.00 or higher). This compares to 27% of those who rated their closest non-work friend in the bottom quartile on this role. Respondents are nearly twice as likely to feel good about their lives if they have a friend to whom they give high ratings on this one role. However, it is not just this one role that relates to SWB. Each role is positively related to SWB. Therefore, each role can contribute to satisfaction with life.

SUMMARY AND APPLICATION

The Vital Friends Assessment is a web-based instrument designed to help individuals discover the roles friends play in their lives. Based on decades of Gallup research on relationships, this instrument is designed to focus on what friends contribute to relationships, not what is missing from the relationships. It is an instrument designed around productive relationships — those consistent with high life satisfaction and high engagement at work.

Participants are asked to select a friendship they would like to evaluate with the assessment. Then the Vital Friends Assessment presents 65 statements that the respondent completes about his or her friend. Once completed, a report is produced that lists the top three Vital Roles the respondent's friend plays in his or her life. Statistically, the themes are ranked according to the extent of respondent endorsement. The Vital Roles offer a measurement-based language to use in describing a friendship that can enable the participant to build on what is right about the relationship.

The Vital Friends Assessment has been rated at the fourth-grade reading level, based on the Flesch-Kincaid Grade Level Formula.

REFERENCES

Carr, J.A. (2006). *A test-retest evaluation of the Vital Friends Assessment.* Omaha, NE: The Gallup Organization.

Diener, E. (1984). Subjective well-being. *Psychological Bulletin, 95,* 542-575.

Harter, J.K., Schmidt, F.L., & Killham, E.A. (2003, July). *Employee engagement, satisfaction, and business-unit-level outcomes: A meta-analysis.* Omaha, NE: The Gallup Organization.

APPENDIX D:
GALLUP RESEARCH ON FRIENDSHIPS

Unless otherwise noted, all research conducted by The Gallup Organization mentioned in this book stems from two primary sources. The first source is the well-known Gallup Poll, the vehicle through which our organization has been gauging world opinions for more than seven decades. The second source is Gallup's rapidly expanding employee engagement database, through which we have asked millions of people how they feel about their workplaces. It is important to note that these two sources represent very different audiences. Gallup conducted the employee engagement surveys for client organizations that contracted with Gallup to measure opinions on a regular basis. In most cases, these studies include a census of employees in a given business unit or organization. In contrast, the data collected via The Gallup Poll is based on a random sampling of anyone 18 years or older within the given population. What follows is a more detailed description of these two major sources of information on friendships.

THE GALLUP POLL

In March 2005, we conducted a poll in which we asked several questions about friendships, life satisfaction, health, and workplace opinions. We surveyed 1,009 people in this specific study. We then compared the data between questions to investigate the linkages between two or more variables. For example, we asked the question: "Overall, how satisfied are you with your life?" early in the survey. And later, we asked people to indicate their level of agreement with the following statement: "My workgroup feels like a family." Respondents rated both items on a 1-5 Likert-type scale. After collecting all the data, we looked for significant linkages between items.

For a detailed explanation of how Gallup Polls are conducted, you can visit the FAQ section at http://www.galluppoll.com.

GALLUP'S EMPLOYEE ENGAGEMENT (Q¹²) DATABASE

In the late 20th century, Gallup scientists realized that we were asking far too many questions when conducting employee surveys. Furthermore, asking different questions in every company and industry was not very helpful for the sake of comparison. As a result, we combed our databases and looked for the most powerful predictors of employee engagement. This resulted in Gallup's Q^{12} metric, which has since been asked of millions of employees worldwide. Of particular interest to our study of friendships was the data accumulated on question 10: "I have a best friend at work."

DATABASE DESCRIPTION

We analyzed data from 2002, 2003, and 2004, which include:

- 4.51 million respondents

- 423,000 workgroups

- 332 clients

- 37 languages

- 112 countries

These data represent 12 major industry types:

- Accommodation and Food Services

- Educational Services

- Finance and Insurance

- Healthcare and Social Assistance

- Information

- Manufacturing

- Professional, Scientific, and Technical Services

- Public Administration

- Retail Trade

- Services

- Services Without Healthcare

- Utilities

THE META-ANALYSIS

A meta-analysis is a statistical integration of data accumulated across many different studies. As such, it provides uniquely powerful information because it controls for measurement and sampling errors and other idiosyncrasies that distort the results of individual studies. A meta-analysis eliminates biases and provides an estimate of true validity or true relationship between two or more variables. Statistics typically calculated during meta-analyses also allow the researcher to explore the presence, or lack thereof, of moderators of relationships.

More than 1,000 meta-analyses have been conducted in the psychological, educational, behavioral, medical, and personnel selection fields. The research literature in the behavioral and social sciences includes a multitude of individual studies with apparently conflicting conclusions. Meta-analysis, however, allows the researcher to estimate the mean relationship between variables and make corrections for artifactual sources of variation in findings across studies. It provides a method by which researchers can ascertain whether validities and relationships generalize across various situations (e.g., across firms or geographical locations).

FINDINGS SPECIFIC TO THE "BEST FRIEND" QUESTION

We found that people with best friends at work have:

- better safety records

- higher customer loyalty scores

- more profitable teams

When people have a best friend at work, they simply achieve more. As we dug deeper into this research, we discovered that employees who report having a best friend at work, when compared to those without a best friend at work, were also:

- 43% more likely to report having received recognition and praise in the previous seven days

- 37% more likely to report that someone at work encourages their development

- 27% more likely to feel that their job aligns with the company's mission

- 27% more likely to feel that their opinions count at work

- 21% more likely to report that at work, they have the opportunity to do what they do best every day

Unfortunately, only 3 in 10 of the millions of people in our database strongly agree that they have a best friend at work, while the remaining 7 in 10 do not. As a result, those who do not strongly agree that they have a best friend at work are drastically less engaged in their jobs: only 8% of these people are engaged. ("Engaged" employees are the people who show up mentally and physically every day and have the highest productivity.)

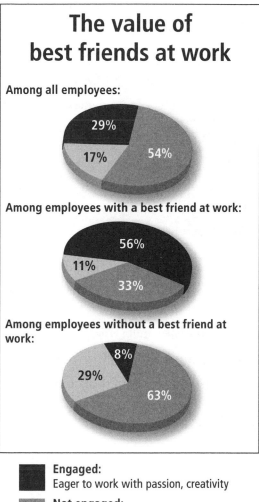

The value of best friends at work

Among all employees:

29%

17% 54%

Among employees with a best friend at work:

56%

11%

33%

Among employees without a best friend at work:

8%

29%

63%

Engaged:
Eager to work with passion, creativity

Not engaged:
Doing minimum work necessary

Actively disengaged:
Undedicated, actively damage productivity

If you do not strongly agree that you have a best friend at work, the chances of being engaged in your job are an abysmal 1 in 12. In sharp contrast, among those who strongly agree that they have a best friend at work, 56% are engaged, and only 11% are actively disengaged. Overall, employees who strongly agree that they have a best friend at work are seven times as likely to be engaged in their work each day.

SUMMARY

This "best friend" item has been, by far, the most controversial part of our standardized employee survey. Every time we prepare to conduct this survey in a new organization or country, people object to this one item and insist that it will not work. However, millions of interviews later, meta-analytic research across a diverse group of companies and countries indicates that this item consistently predicts critical business outcomes.

REFERENCES

Harter, J.K., Schmidt, F.L. & Killham, E.A. (2003, July). *Employee engagement, satisfaction, and business-unit-level outcomes: A meta-analysis*. Omaha, NE: The Gallup Organization.

NOTES

Vital Friends is the product of many great minds. Without the connections between the work of myriad scientists and thinkers, this book would not exist. From the groundbreaking research of Nobel Prize-winning psychologist Daniel Kahneman to the masterful storytelling of journalist Jon Meacham, many thought leaders influenced and shaped this book, and a few of them are mentioned directly in these pages. In these instances, the page number and a short phrase corresponding to each reference in the text are listed below.

Please note that any statistics *not* cited in this section stem from Gallup research and/or studies conducted specifically for publication in this book. This work was the product of several strong connections within our own research labs. If you would like more information about how these data were collected, go to Appendix D.

PART ONE: FRIENDS IN LIFE

CHAPTER 2: THE ENERGY *BETWEEN*

18 *During this time*: Meacham, J. (2003). *Franklin and Winston: An intimate portrait of an epic friendship*. New York: Random House.

CHAPTER 3: BETTER THAN PROZAC?

21 *For starters, scientists have found that friends are catalysts*: Kahneman, D., Krueger, A.B., Schkade, D.A., Schwarz, N., & Stone, A.A. (2004, December 3). A survey method for characterizing daily life experience: The day reconstruction method. *Science, 306*, 1776-1780.

21 *They learned that even the dreaded commute to work is tolerable*: Kahneman, D. (2002). A day in the lives of 1,000 working women in Texas. Presented at the First International Positive Psychology Summit, Washington, D.C.

21 *Perhaps most importantly*: Reis, H.T., & Gable, S.L. (2003). Toward a positive psychology of relationships. In C.L.M. Keyes, & J. Haidt (Eds.), *Flourishing: Positive psychology and*

the life well-lived (pp. 129-159). Washington, D.C.: American Psychological Association.

22 *During our teenage years*: Larson, R., Zuzanek, J., & Mannell, R. (1985). Being alone versus being with people: Disengagement in the daily experience of older adults. *Journal of Gerontology, 40,* 375-381.

22 *Scientists are also uncovering*: Shah, J. (2003). The motivational looking glass: How significant others implicitly affect goal appraisals. *Journal of Personality and Social Psychology, 85,* 424-439.

22 *A 2003 study*: Fitzsimons, G.M., & Bargh, J.A. (2003). Thinking of you: Nonconscious pursuit of interpersonal goals associated with relationship partners. *Journal of Personality and Social Psychology, 84,* 148-164.

24 *...studies are now revealing*: Uno, D., Uchino, B.N., & Smith, T.W. (2002). Relationship quality moderates the effect of social support given by close friends on cardiovascular reactivity in women. *International Journal of Behavioral Medicine, 9,* 243-262.

25 *In a 2001 study*: Brummett, B.H., Barefoot, J.C., Siegler, I.C., Clapp-Channing, N.E., Lytle, B.L., Bosworth, H.B., et al. (2001). Characteristics of socially isolated patients with

coronary artery disease who are at elevated risk for mortality. *Psychosomatic Medicine, 63,* 267-272.

26 *"Friendship has a profound effect on your physical well-being"*: Fisher, P. (Ed.). (1994). *Age erasers for women: Actions you can take right now to look younger and feel great.* New York: St. Martin's Press.

CHAPTER 4: THE SILVER LINING IN A MARRIAGE

28 *British economist Nick Powdthavee*: Hitti, M. (2005, March 22). Recipe for happiness in marriage. *WebMD Medical News.* Retrieved March 23, 2005, from http://my.webmd.com/content/Article/102/106708.htm

28 *In fact, a 2005 study*: Kiecolt-Glaser, J.K., Loving, T.J., Stowell, J.R., Malarkey, W.B., Lemeshow, S., Dickinson, S.L., et al. (2005). Hostile marital interactions, proinflammatory cytokine production, and wound healing. *Archives of General Psychiatry, 62,* 1377-1384.

28 *According to Professor Jan Kiecolt-Glaser*: myDNA News. (2005, December 9). Bad marriages: Unhealthy? Retrieved January 20, 2006, from http://www.mydna.com/resources/news/news_20051209_marriage_stress_healing.html

29 *You have probably heard this alarming statistic before*: Americans for Divorce Reform. (n.d.). Divorce rates. Retrieved August 19, 2005, from http://www.divorcereform.org/rates. html

29 *According to Dr. John Gottman*: Gottman, J.M., & Silver, N. (1999). *The seven principles for making marriage work: A practical guide from the country's foremost relationship expert.* New York: Three Rivers Press.

CHAPTER 6: DOES WORK BALANCE LIFE?

39 *"Balance is bunk!"*: Hammonds, K.H. (2004, October). Balance is bunk! *Fast Company, 87,* 68-76.

41 *A recent study revealed*: Judge, T.A., & Ilies, R. (2004). Affect and job satisfaction: A study of their relationship at work and at home. *Journal of Applied Psychology, 89,* 661-673.

41 *"The boundaries between work and family"*: Keen, C. (2004, December 2). Employees bring bad moods home, but they disappear by morning. Retrieved February 20, 2006, from University of Florida News website: http://news.ufl. edu/2004/12/02/jobmoods/

PART TWO: FRIENDS AT WORK

CHAPTER 7: THE THREE-FRIEND THRESHOLD

51 *New studies suggest*: Markiewicz, D., Devine, I., & Kausilas, D. (2000). Friendships of women and men at work: Job satisfaction and resource implications. *Journal of Managerial Psychology, 15*, 161-184.

56 *According to some research*: Riordan, C.M., & Griffeth, R.W. (1995). The opportunity for friendship in the workplace: An underexplored construct. *Journal of Business and Psychology, 10*, 141-154.

CHAPTER 8: CAN YOU BE FRIENDS WITH YOUR BOSS?

59 *"Managers learn in business school"*: London, S. (2004, November 15). Drucker managed to do it first [Electronic version]. *Financial Times*.

59 *When compared to time spent with relatives*: Kahneman, D., Krueger, A.B., Schkade, D.A., Schwarz, N., & Stone, A.A. (2004, December 3). A survey method for characterizing daily life experience: The day reconstruction method. *Science, 306*, 1776-1780.

63   *The bottom line is*: Kahneman, D., Krueger, A.B., Schkade, D.A., Schwarz, N., & Stone, A.A. (2004, December 3). A survey method for characterizing daily life experience: The day reconstruction method. *Science, 306*, 1776-1780.

CHAPTER 9: GETTING ENGAGED AT WORK

65   *"Best friendships are good for business."*: Jones, D. (2004, December 1). Best friends good for business [Electronic version]. *USA Today.*

65   *In a recent newspaper interview*: Jones, D. (2004, December 1). Best friends good for business [Electronic version]. *USA Today.*

PART FOUR: BUILDING VITAL FRIENDSHIPS AT WORK

CHAPTER 13: THE WATER COOLER EFFECT

142   *They knew it would take a very innovative design*: Perkins+Will. (n.d.). Best Buy corporate headquarters. Retrieved August 19, 2005, from http://www.perkinswill.com/projects/project.aspx?id=68d

PARTING THOUGHTS

154 *A 2001 study*: DukeMed News. (2004, April 13). Isolated heart patients have twice the risk of dying, present challenges to health care workers. Retrieved August 19, 2005, from http://www.emaxhealth.com/39/176.html

APPENDIXES AND REFERENCES

APPENDIX A: YOUR QUESTIONS

164 *One study found*: Ebbesen, E.B., Kjos, G.L., & Konecni, V.J. (1976). Spatial ecology: Its effects on the choice of friends and enemies. *Journal of Experimental Social Psychology, 12,* 505-518.

APPENDIX B: A CASE STUDY: CAN LEADERS SET THE TONE?

171 *Ford was also known to have his own private army*: Fast Company Staff. (2005, July). Bosses from hell [Electronic version]. *Fast Company, 96,* 47.

173 *In her book* Life on the Line: De Santis, S. (1999). *Life on the line: One woman's tale of work, sweat, and survival.* New York: Doubleday.

174 *Following a 2005 incident*: McKinnon, J.M. (2005, May 29). Contents under pressure: 4 months after shootings, Jeep still seems tense [Electronic version]. *The Blade.*

175 *When Toyota opened its first wholly owned and operated plant in Georgetown*: Maynard, M. (2003). *The end of Detroit: How the big three lost their grip on the American car market.* New York: Doubleday.

SUGGESTED READING

Anderson, C., Keltner, D., & John, O.P. (2003). Emotional convergence between people over time. *Journal of Personality and Social Psychology, 84,* 1054-1068.

Blanchflower, D.G., & Oswald, A.J. (2000). Well-being over time in Britain and the USA. National Bureau of Economic Research. Working Paper 7487.

Ekman, P. (2003). *Emotions revealed: Recognizing faces and feelings to improve communication and emotional life.* New York: Times Books.

Larson, R.W., & Bradney, N. (1988). Precious moments with family members and friends. In R.M. Milardo (Ed.), *Families and social networks* (pp. 107 126). Newbury Park, CA: Sage Publications.

Pennebaker, J.W. (1990). *Opening up: The healing power of expressing emotions.* New York: William Morrow.

ACKNOWLEDGEMENTS

As I write this, I am sitting on the deck of a log cabin in Montana, looking out over a snowcapped mountain range and the Yellowstone River. The setting is picturesque and serene. But the beauty of the scenery is less significant to me than the fact that I am enjoying it with three of the most important people in my life — three of my vital friends.

On the left, my 82-year-old grandmother, Shirley, is leaning against a wooden railing, looking off into the distance, hoping to spot another family of deer on the riverbank. This loving mother of four simply radiates warmth. When I was young, Shirley cared for me every afternoon, taught me how to read, and above all else, truly was my best friend. When I stop and think about what my grandmother has contributed to my life, it is hard to imagine how anyone could compare — but her eldest daughter, my mother, Connie, does. She has always been the ultimate developer of people, and she has a keen ability to listen in a way that makes you feel as if her entire life were dedicated to improving yours. Seated to my mother's right is my wife, Ashley. Her contagious spirit and smile could illuminate even the darkest of places. I have learned a great deal by observing the way Ashley's energy, depth, and sincerity have built powerful friendships. As I continue to reflect, it is easy to see how these vital friendships have profoundly shaped my life, for which I am eternally grateful.

I have happily experienced a great deal of overlap between my personal and professional lives. This book was inspired by my late grandfather, colleague, and mentor, Don Clifton, who first suggested that we spend more time studying "what was right" in the late 1960s.

Perhaps most importantly, it took thousands of Gallup employees and client partners to build the massive research base described in this book. When I gathered the Vital Friends research team for the first time, this research base allowed us to review more than eight million interviews . . . before we even got started. The core team — Bret Bickel, Jim Harter, Tim Hodges, Amanda Jedlicka, Dalia Mogahed, and Sujatha Mukundan — was responsible for the research and insights contained in

Vital Friends. This group of co-authors and co-inventors not only made this book much stronger, but also made working on the project fun. They are some of the most gifted scientists and thinkers I have known.

As always, Geoff Brewer, Kelly Henry, and Piotrek Juszkiewicz made the book much stronger. This brilliant core team worked tirelessly to make *Vital Friends* a reality. These are the three people I would never want to write a book without. In addition, the high-level guidance and encouragement from Jim Clifton and Larry Emond kept everything headed in the right direction.

Other key people throughout the development of this book were Jason Carr and Mark Stiemann, who double-checked all of our facts and numbers; Kim Goldberg, who guided the book's layout; David Osborne and Kathleen Hinton, who helped me compile feedback and sources; and Emily Meyer, who kept things moving forward as time went on. Barbara Cave Henricks, our publicist, also deserves special thanks for her shrewd advice and for helping us to reach as wide an audience as possible. She and the rest of Lynn Goldberg's team at Goldberg McDuffie are the best in the business. And a very special thanks to Rachel Penrod for maximizing my time with perfection as I worked through various drafts.

In addition, the following team led the creation of the action items and strategies in Part Three: Cathy DeWeese, Rod Karr,

Mike Kinney, Curt Liesveld, Jan Meints, Laura Mussman, Jeannie Ruhlman, and Rosemary Travis.

And the Vital Friends website was created by this group of technology gurus: Kate Armstrong, Josh Christensen, Kim Ideus, Swati Jain, Matt Johnson, Jesse McConnell, Tye OsBurn, Stephanie Oswald, Christopher Purdy, David Seevers, Keerat Sharma, Sam Snyder, and Sheri Widler.

Gallup's interviewing center managers and their teams were also central to our efforts. They enabled us to survey thousands of people during the creation of this book. They are: Doug Barlow, Jenny Higgins, Matt Kurtz, Pat Michael, John Ogren, Seth Schuchman, Stephanie Soucie, and Steve Stonebraker.

One thing I have learned about writing, especially when a draft starts out as rough as mine do, is that you can never have enough people involved in reviewing and creating a book, as it always yields a better result. So I would like to offer my thanks to each of the following people, all of whom have left their mark on *Vital Friends*: Vandana Allman, Jim Asplund, Kelly Aylward, Susie Banta, Dana Baugh, Cheryl Beamer, Randy Beck, Kathi Beebe, Sandy Boozer, Brian Brim, Irene Burklund, Scot Caldwell, Anna Chan, Donna Chlopak, Jules Clement, Curt Coffman, Charlie Colón, Barry Conchie, Bob Condello, Bev Conroy, Kirk Cox, Julie Curd, Larry Curd, Chad Davis, Laurie Dean, Tim Dean, Renay Dey, Dan Draus, Fabricio Drumond, Mark Eberly,

Eldin Ehrlich, Sherry Ehrlich, Peter Flade, Tonya Fredstrom, Jennie Glass, Jeya Govindarajan, Kreg Green, Barb Griess, Christy Hammer, Becky Hanna, Dave Harbuck, Molly Hardin, Ty Hartman, Tom Hatton, Ted Hayes, Sonny Hill, Maggie Hoppe, Jamie Hunt, Rachel Johanowicz, Mark John, Emily Killham, Julie Kohrell, Jerry Krueger, Mark Lacey, Julie Lamski, Tosca Lee, Rosanne Liesveld, Shane Lopez, Marc Lovci, Mary Penner-Lovci, Allison Lowry, Michael Lowry, Sharon Lutz, Carolyn Madison, Shannon Marullo, Charles McClendon, Kevin McConville, Tara McGhee, Jacque Merritt, Jan Miller, Jane Miller, Jo Ann Miller, Ronny Miller, Ariel Mink, Gabriel Gonzalez-Molina, Mike Morrison, Sue Munn, Jacques Murphy, Grant Mussman, Eric Nielsen, Terry Noel, Steve O'Brien, Shannon O'Keefe, Eric Olesen, Jil Owen, Morgen Paul, Rod Penner, Evan Perkins, Paul Petters, Sarah Piccin, Joy Plemmons, Mark Pogue, Adam Pressman, Mary Reckmeyer, Jillene Reimnitz, Leslie Rowlands, Mike Rude, Steve Ruedisili, Pam Ruhlman, Barb Sanford, Yvonne Sen, Catherine Shada, Steph Sharma, Cheryl Siegman, Kim Simeon, Todd Smith, Brenda Sonksen, Cheryl Steele, Phil Stone, Jen Stonebraker, Joe Streur, Rob Sturgis, Charlie Thomas, Debbie Toto, Ella Turrentine, Julie VanDerwerken, Jeanne Weisbrook, Jim Wells, Mindy Wells, Tobi Wenzl, Brian Weyant, Jim Whitmore, Yvette Wiebe, Kryste Wiedenfeld, Sam Wolman, Jane Wood, John Wood, Al Woods, Heather Wright, Warren Wright, Yongwei Yang, and Amy Zuckerman.

In closing, I want to thank the vital friends who have brought so much to my life. From long-term friends to the family members and colleagues who continue to make an impact, I offer my most sincere thanks and gratitude. You are the friends who make life fulfilling . . . and fun.

LEARN MORE

- Programs, consulting, and measurement that focus on building vital friendships in your organization.

- Vital Friends workshops designed for your company, school, or faith-based organizations.

- Share your stories about great vital friendships or illustrations of the eight Vital Roles in action.

Visit our website at www.vitalfriends.com

Contact us by e-mail at vf@gallup.com

About the Author

Tom Rath is coauthor of the #1 *New York Times* and #1 *BusinessWeek* bestseller, *How Full Is Your Bucket?* With more than 500,000 copies in print within its first year of publication, his book has spent 15 months on the domestic bestseller list. Now available in more than 10 languages, Rath's book has also been an international bestseller.

After 12 years with The Gallup Organization, Rath now leads Gallup's Workplace Research and Leadership Consulting worldwide. He also serves on the board of VHL.org, an organization dedicated to cancer research and patient support.

Rath earned his bachelor's degree in psychology from the University of Michigan. He is currently pursuing graduate degrees at Johns Hopkins University and the University of Pennsylvania. He lives in Washington, D.C.